ACCESSING THE SUPERINTENDENCY

ACCESSING THE SUPERINTENDENCY
The Unwritten Rules

Marilyn Tallerico

A joint publication of the
American Association of School Administrators
and Corwin Press, Inc.

CORWIN PRESS, INC.
A Sage Publications Company
Thousand Oaks, California

For information:

Corwin Press, Inc.
A Sage Publications Company
2455 Teller Road
Thousand Oaks, California 91320
E-mail: order@corwinpress.com

SAGE Publications Ltd.
6 Bonhill Street
London EC2A 4PU
United Kingdom

SAGE Publications India Pvt. Ltd.
M-32 Market
Greater Kailash I
New Delhi 110 048 India

Printed in the United States of America

Library of Congress Cataloging-in-Publication Data

Tallerico, Marilyn.
    Accessing the superintendency: the unwritten rules / Marilyn Tallerico.
    p. cm.
Includes bibliographical references (p.   ) and index.
    ISBN 0-8039-6895-7 (alk. paper) — ISBN 0-8039-6896-5 (pbk.: alk. paper)
    I. Title. 1. School superintendents—Selection and appointment—
United States.
    LB2831.752 .T38 2000
    371.2'011

99-006843

This book is printed on acid-free paper.

00   01   02   03   04   05   10   9   8   7   6   5   4   3   2   1

Production Editor: S. Marlene Head
Editorial Assistant: Kylee Liegl
Typesetter: Rebecca Evans
Cover Designer: Michelle Lee

Contents

Part II: Preventing and Promoting Advancement

Acknowledgments

I am indebted to the school board members, superintendents, candidates for superintendencies, and search consultants whose candor, insights, and perspectives helped inform this research. Special, heartfelt appreciation is also extended to Joan N. Burstyn and Chris Ritter, for their unwavering support and encouragement. I thank the anonymous reviewers of the manuscript, whose suggestions and thoughtful critique helped hone this book. I am grateful to Dean Steven T. Bossert and Syracuse University, for awarding the research leave that facilitated this project. Finally, I wish to thank the editorial and production teams at Corwin Press, whose skills and assistance were essential to this volume.

* * *

Corwin Press would like to acknowledge the following reviewers:

Maenette K. P. Benham
College of Education
Michigan State University
Lansing, MI

Margo Marvin
Windsor Locks Public Schools
Windsor Locks, CT

Alrita Morgan
East Penn School District
Emmaus, PA

Flora Ida Ortiz
School of Education
University of California, Riverside
Riverside, CA

Stephen Rowley
Bainbridge Island School District #303
Bainbridge Island, WA

Linda Tinelli Shieve
Educational Administration Department
Oswego State University of New York
Oswego, NY

William D. Silky
Educational Administration Department
Oswego State University of New York
Oswego, NY

Barbara Smith
Department of Education
Radford University
Radford, VA

About the Author

Marilyn Tallerico has published widely in the areas of gender and politics in public school educational leadership. She has researched superintendent–school board relationships, women in the superintendency, urban school governance, and other issues related to promoting diversity, equity, and excellence in educational administration. She coauthored the monograph *Gender and Politics at Work: Why Women Exit the Superintendency*, and she coedited the book *City Schools: Leading the Way*. Her work has appeared in more than a dozen educational journals, including *Educational Administration Quarterly, Journal of School Leadership, Qualitative Sociology, Urban Education*, and the *Journal of Staff Development*. Her previous research has been supported by the Educational Foundation of the American Association of University Women (AAUW), the National Policy Board on Educational Administration (NPBEA), and the New York State Association for Women in Administration.

During her 25 years in education, Tallerico has been a central office curriculum administrator, a coordinator of bilingual and English-as-a-Second-Language programs, and a Spanish teacher. Currently, she is Associate Professor of Educational Leadership at Syracuse University. She teaches graduate courses in staff development, assessment of teaching, curriculum leadership, politics of education, and supervision. She has served as visiting professor at Pennsylvania State University, and she was assistant to the Executive Director of the University Council for Educational Administration (UCEA). She is active in numerous organizations and has presented papers at scores of national and regional conferences.

Tallerico earned her PhD in educational leadership at Arizona State University and her master's and undergraduate degrees at the University of Connecticut. In addition to her professional interests, she is an avid tennis player, a fledgling golfer, and a happy traveler.

Introduction

You've probably applied for employment in the public schools before. You've likely obtained several positions in education. Sometimes, friends or acquaintances have helped you get a foot in the door. Other times, you've done it alone: completing applications, interviewing with administrators, and, perhaps, meeting with selection committees of teachers and parents.

Accessing the superintendency is different. School board members are directly and intensely involved. The search and selection process can take 8 to 18 months. The superintendency is the one position for which school boards frequently engage the services of outside facilitators. You've heard these people or firms referred to as headhunters or search consultants. All in all, a different mix of powerholders and procedures come into play, compared to accessing other teaching and leadership positions.

The superintendency is also unique because it's been the slowest of all K-12 administrative roles to integrate women and people of color. What's gender got to do with obtaining a superintendency? What about race and ethnicity? How do school boards and headhunters find and select superintendents? What occurs behind the scenes? How do headhunters think? Why do school boards operate as they do? And what does all this mean for current and prospective administrators who are the future pool of superintendent applicants? These are the questions this book addresses.

Whether you are a graduate student of educational leadership or a practicing administrator, you will get an inside look at common superintendent selection practices. Thereby, you will be better prepared both to access the superintendency yourself one day and to lead the systemic changes needed to increase diversity in the field overall. You will acquire a thorough understanding of the invisible

1

selection criteria, the unwritten rules, and the gender and other biases that can affect access to this important educational leadership position. You will learn how current practices both help and hinder the advancement of women and other nontraditional candidates to the superintendency.

Sure, many of you have heard war stories from colleagues about the politics of superintendent selection. You may have acquired considerable anecdotal information about the equity and diversity issues involved. This book, however, relies on systematic research. It combines syntheses of prior investigations with an original study that draws upon the firsthand experiences of 75 headhunters, school board members, and recent candidates for superintendencies. These are the people closest to current superintendent search and selection practices. Their thinking and experiences reveal insights about many of the key processes that are invisible to the public (e.g., consultants' telephone recruiting, confidential reference checking, school board executive sessions, and private interviews with candidates). It is behind the scenes where gender and other biases are exercised. (You can read more about these data sources in the Appendix on Research Methods.)

Why is it important to increase your understanding of accessing the superintendency and the diversity issues involved? One reason is that the immediate future ensures abundant superintendent vacancies—and, therefore, opportunities for you. A majority of the nation's 15,000 school districts will need to hire a new superintendent within the next 5 to 7 years (Glass, 1992).

A second reason is that there are record numbers of women in graduate preparation programs and in administrative positions that can be stepping stones to the superintendency (Grogan, 1996). There are also record numbers of children of color enrolled in America's schools (Jackson, 1995). The kinds of gender/racial/ethnic analyses contained in this book are typically absent from educational administration texts, yet they provide useful insights and illustrations for future candidates.

Description of the Book

What, more specifically, will you find in this volume? Part I includes three chapters, all aimed at bringing to light common superintendent search and selection practices. Chapter 1, "How Do School Boards Prepare for the Search?" explains why boards engage the services of consultants and how community groups can be involved. It illustrates how advertised qualifications are developed and why they do not always reflect actual selection priorities. For example, published criteria may be designed for their public relations value to board constituencies, or to preclude or promote the candidacy of an insider.

Chapter 2, "What Is Recruiting and Interviewing Candidates All About?" describes what prospective applicants should know about the different forms of active and passive recruitment, and team- or single-consultant screening interviews. This chapter also identifies common types of interview questions and the kinds of background inquiries made about applicants. It emphasizes the hypervaluing of "intangibles, gut, and chemistry" in final interviews.

The third chapter, "How Are Hiring and Powerbrokering Related?" examines several of the most anxiety-producing issues for superintendency applicants: communication during the search and selection process, the time it takes, confidentiality, and board dissensus. I argue that, although the players in superintendency powerbrokering appear to have changed during this century, the system remains largely intact. This chapter identifies the factors that contribute to that system's enduring strengths, such as boards' reliance on consultants and their networks to narrow the field for them, and the interpretive leeway in screening allowed by both the unwritten criteria that come into play and the breadth of stated qualifications hoped for in candidates.

Taken together, the three chapters that make up Part I provide background and understanding of the specific steps involved in superintendent search and selection, along with their implications for prospective candidates. This sets the stage for the gender and diversity analyses that are the focus of the four chapters in Part II.

Chapter 4, "What Do Sex and Color Have to Do With It?" introduces broader sociopolitical factors that superintendent search and selection practices both reflect and reinforce. For example, it examines how current optimism about recent gains made by women and people of color, distaste for affirmative action, and faith in gender neutrality and color blindness combine to reinforce the American ideal that the best qualified individuals rise naturally to the top. This chapter illustrates how "best qualified" is defined, with respect to viable candidacy for the superintendency, and why these definitions disadvantage women and people of color.

The next chapter exposes how and where both overt and subtle biases affect access to the superintendency. Examples include questions such as: Is this district ready for a woman? Can she be tough enough? With whom can the board work most "naturally"? Other illustrations reflect taken-for-granted assumptions that the successor superintendent will be a married, white male with school-aged children. This chapter identifies strategies that candidates use to deal with prejudicial inquiries and biases. It also discusses the pros and cons of these approaches.

Chapter 6, "How Do Consultants and School Boards Help?" looks at what key gatekeepers do to challenge norms, remove historic obstacles to women and minorities, and open up superintendent search and selection processes to a diverse range of educational leaders. This chapter stresses what current and future school administrators can learn from these promising practices.

The next chapter also focuses on the positive and proactive. Chapter 7 recommends ways to connect with and influence the informal administrator networks important to obtaining superintendencies. It shares insights on how to find mentors for different purposes, create opportunities to expand current skills, and ensure that personal accomplishments become known beyond the immediate community.

The book concludes by recapping major themes and challenging current and future administrators to play a role in improving selection practices. This chapter, titled "So What?" moves the book beyond practical utility for personal career advancement and underscores moral implications for the educational leadership profession.

Summary and Use

Three premises underlie this volume. First, there are regularities to superintendent search and selection that, although often invisible to the public, can be brought to light and demystified. Second, gender biases and other unwritten rules present unique challenges for women and others who are unlike most incumbent, white, male superintendents. Third, understanding the stated and unstated norms of selection can lead to successfully accessing the superintendency.

This book will let you in on the "hows" and the "whys" of superintendent selection, while simultaneously questioning who benefits from current practices.

The portrait that this volume paints is a composite. That is, it is based on original case study data supplemented by syntheses of existing theory and research. When "this study" is referred to, or vignettes and direct quotations from school board members, consultants, and candidates are used, you can assume that they are from the original case study. Other researchers' findings and theories will always be accompanied by their last names and year of publication, with complete citations in the list of references at the back of this volume.

All informants for the case study were promised anonymity in reporting results. Throughout the book, therefore, pseudonyms are used for individuals and school districts. Where necessary to preserve confidentiality, identifying details have been changed. The terms "headhunters," "search consultants," and "consultants" are used interchangeably throughout and refer to both individuals and search firms.

Other Audiences and Uses for This Book

Although the primary audience for this volume is K-12 educational administrators and students in graduate-level educational leadership preparation programs—the future pool of superintendents—others will find this research useful as well.

Professors of educational administration will likely value the in-depth examination of current practice and the gender and diversity analyses typically absent from school leadership textbooks. This volume can be used as a supplementary reader in courses such as "The Superintendency," "The Politics of Education," or "Gender and Educational Leadership."

Women's studies scholars will find that this research enriches our understanding of subtle forms of sexism that operate just below the surface of conventional practice in a specific profession. In this instance, the particular field is K-12 educational administration, a context that affects virtually all children in the United States.

For readers who are school board members or consultants, this book will identify and illustrate a number of variations in superintendent search and selection procedures. Those of you familiar with just a single approach will find these variations of great interest. For example, you may find useful the illustrations of different ways that community groups can be included or not, and the practices that tend to preclude or promote diversity in the potential pool of applicants.

A Final Thought

Although this book demystifies a largely invisible process, it also offers prospects for change: It identifies ways to be inclusive and to promote access to the superintendency by equitably tapping all available talent pools. You, too, can become a part of these important changes.

Part I

Demystifying the Process

1

How Do School Boards Prepare for the Search?

Jo-Ann Hogan, a school board member, talks about superintendent selection as the most exciting and the most terrifying part of board work. She should know. She's done it four times during her 19 years of service for the Evreeton school district.

According to Jo-Ann, it's exciting because it's a time for the board to revisit what it wants for the community's children and what it expects of the school district's administrative leadership. It's terrifying because the search itself is long, labor intensive, and, in the end, "You're always left wondering, Was this really the best person out there? Did they really do everything they could to find us the top people?" The "they" she refers to are the consultants employed to assist the board in executing its search and selection. "Once we tried to do it by ourselves, but it took too much of the board's time and energies. The other three times, we hired headhunters to do a lot of the work. It's complicated. There are so many steps involved, and each one has to be done well to keep the process moving along."

Diane Devin, a veteran school administrator who recently obtained her first superintendency, wishes there had been a course in her university's preparation program titled "Job Access 101." It would explain "all the steps you have to go through to get a superintendency." In Diane's experience, "It took me a half-dozen tries. And to tell you the truth, I was clueless the first two times through. Then, I started to see some patterns. And to understand why you'd spend so much time [as an applicant] waiting. There's so much that goes on behind the scenes, by the boards, the consultants, and the other players you don't even know about until later."

9

What exactly are the steps in this process considered so arduous by school boards and so mysterious to prospective candidates? Although superintendent search and selection practices vary by both district and consultant, there is a remarkable sameness to the strategies employed and the general flow of the process (Afton, 1985; Magowan, 1979; Radich, 1992; Rickabaugh, 1986; Roberts, 1996; Swart, 1990). (See Figure 1.1 at end of this chapter.) The most common activities involved may be grouped into seven broad categories: initial preparations for the search, advertisement and recruitment for the position, preliminary screening of candidates by the consultant, narrowing the field of candidates by the board or its designees, in-district interviews of semifinalists, selection of finalists, and hiring (Kamler, 1995; Kamler & Shakeshaft, 1998; Martin, 1978; Ortiz, 1998; Tieman, 1968).

This chapter explores the first of these stages: preparing for the search. You will learn from board members why they hire search consultants to help find superintendent candidates, and how they decide among the various consultants available: national search firms, individual entrepreneurs, regional superintendents, university-based headhunters, retired superintendents, or school board associations. You will see how community groups and committees can be involved at this stage to provide information to boards and consultants about district needs, goals, and directions. You will read telling examples of the kinds of private conversations that go into identifying the district's stated and unstated profiles of desired candidate qualities. Most importantly, you will come to understand the significance of these preparatory activities for future applicants.

To Search or Not to Search?

Once it is apparent to a school board that it will need to hire a new superintendent, one of the first determinations it makes is whether there is a logical successor to the incumbent within the district. If there is, a search would not be needed—and you would not have the opportunity to apply. Of course, the presence of an internal candidate does not guarantee appointment without an advertised search.

There were several instances in this study where internal candidates were required to compete with outside applicants in a conventional search process. There were also instances in which consultant-assisted searches were concluded and the board's dissatisfaction with the external candidates who emerged caused them to value a particular insider more highly than before. This, too, could lead to an internal appointment. As one school board member put it, "Sometimes, you just don't know until you look around and see what's out there."

Although it's unclear exactly how distant "out there" is, national data indicate that about 36% are promoted to superintendent from within their own district, down from 38% in 1982 (Glass, 1992). A more recent study in New York indicates that about 70% of superintendents are appointed from outside the employing district, whereas 27% are promoted from within (Volp et al., 1998).

What does all this mean for you? Regardless of the administrative position you occupy or aspire to next, don't count on being promoted to the superintendency in your current school system. Odds are two-to-one in favor of your school board deciding to hire someone from outside the district. So, if your goal is to obtain a superintendency, be prepared to change school districts.

Who Will Facilitate the Search?

Okay. The board has determined that a search is needed. Its next decision is whether or not it wishes to conduct the search process itself or with the assistance of a consultant or other outside facilitator. In practice, local boards often confer with either their regional superintendent or the state school board association to come to this decision. Sometimes, the exiting superintendent, a neighboring school district superintendent, a nearby university professor, or board members from other school systems may also help the board think this through. Less frequently, national professional associations of administrators or school boards are sought out for their advice.

Previous research has shown that school boards are relying more and more on consultant-assisted searches rather than district-based search teams (Magowan, 1979; Rickabaugh, 1986; Swart, 1990; Tieman, 1968). For example, Tieman (1968) surveyed 239 board presidents and 37 consultants in two midwestern states. He found a greater use of consultants in the 1960s than in the 1950s. Swart's (1990) more recent study of a northeastern state found that the percentage of superintendent searches relying on district-based search teams (rather than outside consultants) declined from 49% in 1975 to 2% in

1990. Rickabaugh (1986) notes that scarcity of corporate leadership talent contributed to the growth of the executive search industry in the private sector. If the same holds true for the superintendency, the reported decline in numbers of applicants per search in the 1990s (O'Connell, 1995) may foreshadow continued increases in school boards' employment of headhunters.

Where do boards find these consultants? Although it depends on the norms and traditions in particular states, local school boards usually have numerous sources of search assistance. These include national search firms, individual entrepreneurs, college- or university-based headhunters, county/regional superintendents, state school board associations, retired superintendents, or consortia of various combinations of any of the above. Typically, boards make their choice among them on the basis of cost, the desired scope of the search, and trust.

With respect to cost, the range is wide and almost constantly changing, depending upon market variations in supply and demand. At the time this study was conducted, costs ranged from a low of about $2,000, including only the consultant's telephone charges, postage, advertisement, printing, and other minor expenses, to a high of about $40,000 for the most prestigious executive search firms.

Although many searches are conducted on a regional or statewide basis, when more distant consulting firms or individuals are hired, the expectation is typically for a nationwide search for an experienced superintendent. Naturally, the base of operation of the national firm brings additional costs. A school board member from an affluent suburban district reports, "In our last search, we spoke with some regional and some national headhunters. One was based in California and another in Chicago. But the thought of paying the transportation costs for each trip here was a little daunting. So, we hired someone from within-state."

As alluded to in this quotation, boards often request proposals and hear presentations from several search service providers. Consultants distinguish what they can bring to a board in various ways. Some cite longevity in the business or frequency of their searches: "I've completed more superintendent searches in this state in the past 10 years than any other private consulting firm." Others cite the reverse, that is, that they are not entrenched in the existing systems and networks and can, therefore, bring fresh perspectives. Some tout their national experience and the increased objectivity that an out-ofstater might bring. In contrast, others capitalize on their proximity, familiarity with the region, or prior service to the board on non-search-related matters.

Some consultants provide numerical data documenting prior leadership stability: "Each of the last six superintendents I assisted in placing remained in their new district at least 7 years." Some vaunt the soundness or thoroughness of the search and selection processes they employ. Others distinguish themselves by their flexibility: "I go in with a series of questions for the board rather than a set process." Some cite the uniqueness of their mixed-sex or mixed-race consulting team to prescreen applicants. Others underscore their personal history and connections: "I've been an educator for 40 years; held every school administrative position there is, from principal through [regional] superintendent; and know people all across this state who can give us good information." Most emphasize their secondary role to the school board's, assuring that "the board will maintain control of the process." Some never actively seek the search consultancy role. Instead, boards with whom they have worked on other consulting projects pursue them and request that they facilitate their superintendent search.

To help sort through these various claims of strengths and distinguishing features, board members sometimes solicit the advice of neighboring school boards and check references provided by the consultants. They seek information about individuals' reputations for running successful searches. They ask questions like, How do you operate? Where can we do background checks on you with other districts? How many candidates will you bring us who match our profile of qualifications?

Interestingly, some of the documents that were circulating among districts and that were analyzed for this study urge board members to consider several key questions before deciding among consultants. For example, will the consultant gain monetarily from being involved in the superintendent selection? What are the consultants' connections with an institution that trains administrators? Does the consultant have the responsibility for placing these administrators in jobs? Will the consultant be objective and truly committed to the welfare of the school district? Does the consultant know what it is like to work with administrators in practice, not just theory?

Embedded in these questions are concerns for professional integrity, conflict of interest, and educational experience. These foci, corroborated in this study's interviews, also suggest a kind of ambivalence or tension: simultaneous wariness and valuing of consultants' connections to the field of practitioners. We'll return to these points a bit later in the chapter.

Why Do Boards Employ Headhunters?

Convenience, expertise, and access to candidate pools are three salient factors in boards' decisions to enlist the assistance of a consultant rather than conduct the search by themselves (Martin, 1978). First, a few words about convenience. With the demanding ongoing workloads of school board members, it is often viewed as practical to outsource the numerous tasks associated with orchestrating a fruitful superintendent search and selection process. Even with the assistance of a consultant, board members emphasize how time-consuming and tiring the review of applications, interviews, and selection decision making are. Additional evening and weekend meetings are involved, often in close proximity to one another so that details stay fresh in reviewers' minds. Consultants "make it easier for us" by narrowing the slate of applicants for the board's consideration. "We knew we wanted a headhunter to go out and not necessarily find the candidate, but find the pool to bring to us." More specifically, boards' workloads are reduced, for example, when they review 10 files resulting from the consultant's weeding out of the 40 to 60 applications that may have been submitted originally.

Also related to convenience and pragmatism, many boards value the facilitation skills of outside consultants, particularly because stakeholder group discussions and board consensus-building are often key pieces of the search and selection process. A board member explained, "It's almost like teacher negotiations. Sometimes, it's good to bring in an outsider who can take all the heat and then walk away."

Expertise is another salient factor in boards' decisions to engage a headhunter. Typically, professional search consultants have more experience with these processes than do most boards. But it's not only a matter of frequency. Consultants build their personal reputations on who they are, how they facilitate the process, and who they place. The issue of reputation-building contributes to boards' faith in headhunters' expertise: "Surely they wouldn't want to ruin that."

Even when there are several veteran school board members with prior experience in hiring a superintendent, there are inevitably newer or novice members also on the board. As an experienced board member explains: "Imagine you're a new school board member with no experience hiring a superintendent!"

Also contributing to the reliance on search consultants' expertise is that some board members feel a bit abandoned, at a loss, or vulnerable, especially if the exiting incumbent superintendent was highly regarded and depended upon by the board. Most boards prefer that their administrative leadership be in place, so the prospect of being leaderless for any amount of time can be unwelcome. In the words of a six-year veteran board member who was involved in a search in her second year on the board: "The board never even considered running the search themselves. They felt helpless, and they felt the need to be led. We wouldn't know where to begin. It's interesting. Knowing where I've been now, I would have argued to at least consider that option."

Related to expertise, and also salient in boards' decisions to engage the assistance of a headhunter, is school board members' understanding that professional consultants are much more familiar than they are with the informal statewide and national networks of potential candidates and nominators of candidates (Kamler, 1995; Rickabaugh, 1986; Swart, 1990). In contrast, many school board members' networks of contacts are limited, especially outside their immediate region. Some board members acknowledge the norms of confidentiality that seem to characterize experienced administrators' and consultants' initial sources of information, background investigation, and leads: "As a board member, how would I make reference checks? Besides, you can't just call anybody. They may not even know the person has applied!"

But, as mentioned earlier, access to existing networks of informants involves both pros and cons in boards' decisions to engage a search consultant. On one hand, there's the acknowledgment that resumés and placement files provide only a partial, largely glowing portrayal of applicants. Boards and consultants are often concerned that "official" references are rarely completely forthcoming. For example, Sullivan's (1997) research in the private sector found that many organizations share incomplete information about applicants out of fear of defamation claims by unsuccessful candidates. Similarly, Half (1985) found that the majority of human resource

professionals and top executives in Fortune 1000 companies are reluctant to be candid about candidates they refer. In education, expectations of a similar lack of candor contribute to a reliance on consultants' informal networks of information providers.

Board members recognize the need for corroboration and investigation of what appears on paper. Thus, the additional data gleaned
through the consultant's network may diminish the hiring board's
risk: "It's more than a matter of just someone going through the
paperwork. You have to have the connections and the network to
learn what's behind what's said on the resumé. Superintendents and
former superintendents have that, as do well-connected, experienced consultants."

Besides its investigative value, access to these networks is also
critical to the active recruitment of prospective candidates (Kamler,
1995; Zakariya, 1987). From a board member's perspective, "Essentially, what you want the consultant to do is have an idea of who's out
there. Who can they go to and say, 'You know, you would make a
very fine superintendent for [X district]. I think they would love you.
I think you would love the district. And I think you should consider
it.' You know, sometimes, you want to recruit someone who is not
looking at the want ads and not even thinking about moving. That's
probably the best reason to get someone who is a good consultant
and who knows who's out there who would be a fit. Maybe it's someone that he or she had placed years before. Maybe it's someone that
he or she knows of through the grapevine."

This same board member, however, is aware that consultants'
connections may have a downside as well: "Then, of course, you
worry about them having their favorites and who they're bringing in
for you to see. You may never get to see some of the great applicants
because they don't become finalists. The deck could be stacked by the
consultant. That is something the board is concerned about, and
that's why we checked out several consultants." Many board member informants echoed these same advantages and disadvantages of
consultants' network access. Some alluded to gender and diversity
as part of these concerns. A school board member cautions, "[The
headhunter's] network is very valuable. It's also very worrisome to
the board in that he may be using it to advance his own favorites. And
the same thing with the superintendent network. I've heard it referred to by several as the 'good ol' boys club.' And we're concerned
about that. We wanted to make sure that we gave equal opportunity

to everybody that applied. But you'd have those same concerns no matter who was helping with the search." Ultimately, although boards may weigh the pros and cons of existing information alliances, many continue to rely on headhunters because their familiarity and access to these networks are seen as key to the development of a quality pool of candidates for consideration.

But access to candidate pools, expertise, and convenience are not the only factors contributing to boards' reliance on outside help for superintendent search and selection. Other norms of school board work are also influential. For example, it is not unusual for boards to engage the assistance of an outside facilitator for other significant decisions, projects, processes, or issues unrelated to superintendent search and selection. These may include school board self-assessment, superintendent-school board team building, board and administrator retreats of various sorts, long-term visioning projects, strategic planning sessions with community representatives, collective bargaining with teachers and/or other staff, or new school board member orientation processes (Konnert & Augenstein, 1990; Leithwood, 1995). In these situations, as with superintendent searches, the assumption is that there is a unique value to outsiders' perspectives. As mentioned earlier, not only can these people walk away after raising or dealing with charged dissensus, but they can also "put a mirror up and say, 'Listen guys, this is what you're saying. Is this really what you want?'"

Moreover, both observation at public meetings and prior research (Danzberger & Usdan, 1992; First & Walberg, 1992; Jackson, 1995; Tallerico, 1989) tell us that the vast majority of school boards are long accustomed to making decisions based on the recommendations or identification of options provided by their superintendent. There is a powerful operational norm of board reliance on the expertise of experienced administrators. This norm may contribute to it seeming natural to likewise seek the counsel and recommendations of professional search consultants in the high-stakes decision of selecting a new superintendent. In addition, it is frequently expected that an outside facilitator will bring a degree of third-party objectivity and dispassionate assessment to what can be one of the most emotional and politically volatile hiring events for a school district.

An additional factor salient in boards' decisions to employ headhunters is trust (or distrust). Trust was mentioned earlier in the discussion about how boards choose among consultants. It is equally important to the decision whether or not to use a search consultant at all. Because this study targeted school board members who had engaged in two or more superintendent search processes, it became apparent that prior experience, either with running the search by themselves or with a particular consultant, influenced the subsequent decision about headhunting assistance. That is, if the prior search didn't produce the results or process for which the board had hoped, board members would look to handling it differently the next time around. Conversely, if it went well and a solid working relationship developed, the board might reengage the same consultant: "We wouldn't have used him again if we didn't trust he would do a good job."

In the end, board members consider their feelings, comfort, and level of trust. As a board member puts it, "It all has to do with fit between the headhunter and the board. A good fit with the headhunter is when they [the headhunters] know what you want and will bring in what you want, and if they can't, they will tell you that. There has to be an awful lot of communication, and it has to be honest."

School board members also consider the consultants' formal proposals or presentations to the board, subsequent questions and answers, and a limited amount of outside information gathering about reputations. A decision is made, and, typically, a contract or formal agreement is signed by both the board and the consultant selected.

Implications for Potential Applicants

Why is it important for you, as a possible superintendent candidate in the future, to understand school boards' thinking and practices about choosing among consultants? First, because a key influence on the board's choice is the headhunter's reputation for successful placements in the past, you need to know that all consultants want to be associated with "stars." Therefore, if there is a significant blemish on your professional record to date—or a skeleton in your closet, as it is more likely to be termed in the field vernacular—be assured that the consultant will learn about it. Similarly, if that same consultant can attract applicants with prior experience in the superintendency, and you do not have such experience, your star will likely shine less brightly to him or her.

If either of these scenarios applies to you, don't waste energy getting angry with particular search consultants who do not advance your candidacy. These factors make you less of a sure bet to consultants who stake their reputations, and their self-marketing to boards, on their ability to bring districts a proven product that is likely to continue to perform well in the future.

A second influence on the board's choice is its feeling of trust in, and comfort with, the headhunter. If, in your conversations or encounters with this same consultant, you find him or her intolerable, boorish, or otherwise unprofessional (as some of the informants for this study found), these might be important signals of the kind of expertise that board prefers to employ. You may want to reconsider whether you wish to work for a board with such judgment.

Finally, Carlson's (1961, 1972) research suggests that when a board searches outside of its own district, the kind of superintendent desired is one who will bring changes to the system, rather than maintain the status quo. The board would have probably promoted from within had it sought only a stabilizing performance (Carlson, 1961, 1972). Are you interested in, and prepared for, implementing innovations in this particular setting? Give careful advance thought to this question.

What Happens Next?

Once the board has selected a consultant, it spends some time up front deciding upon search logistics before advertisement or solicitation of prospective candidates. This explains the delays that sometimes occur between the time you may learn of a superintendent's impending exit and the official announcement of the vacancy.

During this period, the consultant is likely helping the board clarify time lines and a calendar for the selection and hiring process, a start-up date for the new superintendent, the need for an interim superintendent to fill any time gaps, a primary contact person on the board for the consultant, the specific salary or salary range to be offered, and the board's preferences regarding residency for the new hire. In some cases, consultants and boards try to anticipate and plan for certain worst case scenarios that might occur in the process. For example, what if board members cannot reach agreement on the best candidate? How will they deal with split votes on finalists?

Salary is often a key issue in these preliminary discussions. Most of the headhunters I interviewed confirmed O'Connell's (1995) findings that consultants believe salary significantly affects the attractiveness of the position and, therefore, the likely quantity and quality of the prospective applicant pool. Some consultants devote considerable energy attempting to influence the board to advertise the highest possible salary; others simply provide the board with information about other administrative salaries in the region and the kinds of prior experiences that can be expected of candidates for different advertised ranges.

The issue of salary is a difficult one for school boards, many of whom are under considerable community pressure to "hold the line" on district spending. Superintendent salaries are often scrutinized by both internal and external stakeholder groups (e.g., teacher associations, taxpayers' organizations). Some states require public disclosure of the superintendent's salary and benefits package; consequently, media attention to these details can be substantial.

In the view of many candidates interviewed for this study, salary was one of several criteria important to them in targeting their applications. However, the reputation of the school board seemed to weigh more heavily in candidates' decisions whether or not to apply for a particular opening. As a prospective future candidate, you need to decide the relative import of each of these factors for yourself. What do you value? What can you live with?

For many boards, the issue of within-district or unrestricted residency for the new hire is also important. Expectations for superintendent visibility and broad-based involvement in the community are high in all types of school systems (Carter & Cunningham, 1997; Crowson, 1987; Danzberger & Usdan, 1992; Institute for Educational Leadership, 1986; Leithwood, 1995). Moreover, in some places, there is the assumption that the highest paid employee of the school district should make an economic contribution to the local community via his or her home investment and consumption of goods and services. These factors contribute to some boards' decisions to require within-district residency for the new hire. Schneider (1998) reports that about 50% of all New York State districts require the superintendent to reside within district boundaries; however, no comparable national data could be found.

In this study, consultants and candidates voice varied opinions about residency requirements. Some agree with the arguments presented above. Others indicate that high standards for visibility and community involvement can be met regardless of home address. And others see within-district residency requirements as an unnecessary constraint on the potential applicant pool. They cite economic conditions that make it difficult to sell existing homes without a financial loss for some applicants. In certain locales, housing is far above the typical affordability scale for many superintendent candidates; for example, in some locations, the average selling price of a home was $350,000 at the time this book was written. A school board member from an affluent district provides a vivid illustration: "This happened with the last superintendent we hired. He had a very nice house in his former district, which he sold for $240,000. He came here and bought a house that was not quite the equivalent, for $600,000. We had to provide a second mortgage for him to enable him to do that." Despite that investment, this board member remains a strong advocate for her district's residency requirement.

In economically poorer areas, available housing may not meet the standards of living to which some superintendent candidates are accustomed. A consultant's experience with a rural school board illustrates this well: "It was a very, very poor, small community. There is no decent housing there for a superintendent. Yet the board wanted residency. I said to them, 'Hey, other than tar paper shacks, there's not a hell of a lot in this district. And whoever's coming in wants a decent home. And if you don't have decent homes, you can't oblige them to live here.'"

Moreover, with the prevalence of dual wage-earners among professional couples, it is impossible for some potential candidates to move their households. A candidate explains, "You have couples now who are both superintendents. What do you do then? If you want to attract the very best, as opposed to someone who's just willing or able to move into the district, you have to be flexible about the superintendent's residency. Do you want the very best candidate? Or do you want the person who can live in the district?" A consultant who likewise advocates for flexibility on this issue reasons, "You don't want to take an already small pool and shrink it. Maybe the people you meet, you would forgive them on residency. But you don't know that at the start of the process. You have to give it a chance to work through the process."

This latter point has important implications for you as a prospective applicant. Even if advertised otherwise, there may ultimately be

room for negotiating residency requirements, should you end up being a favorite of the school board.

Besides salary, residency, and logistical determinations about
time lines, boards usually make two other substantive decisions at
this initial preparation stage: how, if at all, it wishes to involve other
people in the selection process, and what the needs and future direction of the district are. Each of these decisions has important implications for your candidacy.

Community involvement. First, it's important to acknowledge the
variety of meanings for "community involvement" in this context.
This study's informants' varied interpretations have to do primarily
with who, how, and when people other than board of education
members will be a part of the selection process. For some boards, this
means the educational community: teachers and administrators
within the district. Other boards add noninstructional staff of different sorts and/or students. Others include parents, as well as representatives of businesses, senior citizens, or the community at large.
Some boards tap existing districtwide steering committees and strategic planning or shared decision-making groups. Other boards
form new groups.

You should be aware that the expectation for community involvement in superintendent search and selection is a relatively recent phenomenon. Tieman's (1968) research found little community
or teacher participation in these processes prior to the 1960s. Baker
(1952) criticized boards for neglecting the opportunity to involve
teachers and community groups in clarifying goals for the district
through superintendent selection processes in the early 1950s. It
seems that the growth of community involvement in superintendent
search and selection from 1970 to the present parallels the overall increase in citizen input and participation in matters of schooling since
the civil rights movement of the late 1960s (Jackson, 1995).

Currently, community groups usually have one or two principal
tasks in the search and selection process. They help identify district
needs and future directions and/or they are involved in candidate
interviews. In this study, however, the language used by some informants calls into question how genuine or meaningful nonboard
group involvement is. For example, a board member explains, "We
set up all these different committees. We wanted the community to

feel involved. We wanted the staff to feel it was their choice too." Several consultants echoed those remarks.

Sometimes, consultants will hold dear a very specific vision of community involvement, will market their services in that manner, and will agree to work only with boards who commit to their preferred means and scope of involving (or not involving) others. For example, one consultant insists that initial interviewing of semifinalist candidates be done by a broad-based group and includes this detail in the contract that the board signs for the search service. Another consultant emphasizes the board's ultimate responsibility for the hire and advises minimizing the involvement of others in screening applicants. Although I will elaborate on interviewing later in this book, the point here is that the decisions about whom to involve and how and when to involve them are made at the initial groundwork stage of board-consultant discussions.

Pulse-taking. Another reason for mentioning community involvement at this juncture is that most consultants conduct some kind of information gathering about district needs and future directions from people other than board members. This may be in the form of a written survey distributed to district employees and/or community residents. Or, it may involve a series of face-to-face discussions between the consultant and either mixed or separate groups of teachers, parents, administrators, community members, noninstructional staff, or others mentioned earlier.

Whether written survey or group discussion, these inquiries often follow a general progression from broad and positive to more focused on future needs, goals, and prospective candidates. For example, questions might begin with the following: What are the strengths and successes of this district? What do you like about the district? What is unique about the district or community that would draw administrators here from other districts? What are you proud of in your school system? Compared to 5 years ago, what three aspects of the district have improved significantly? What do you think your district does very well?

These sorts of questions are followed with additional questions: What are some of the challenges and issues facing your schools? What's needed in this district? What would you like to see happening in the district in the future? What three major goals would you like to see the district accomplish in the next 3 to 5 years? What things in your school system would you like to see improved?

Finally, questions move toward implications of the previous responses for the individual to be hired. For example: What kind of individual is going to help you attain your vision for this district? What are you looking for in your new superintendent? What special skills, abilities, qualities, background, experiences, and training would help the new superintendent be successful here?

Consultants underscore the importance of structuring stakeholder input in this sequence in order to avoid employment criteria grounded in simplistic comparisons with the exiting superintendent. That is, they seek to base the search on district needs and desired future directions, rather than on the deficiencies or strengths of the predecessor. Informants report a natural tendency for the community to want either a clone of the exiting superintendent (if he or she remains highly regarded) or the exact opposite (if he or she has fallen out of their good graces).

Typically, the consultant summarizes findings from all of these inquiries and brings this information to the school board for its consideration. Board deliberation of these same (or similar) questions may occur prior to, simultaneous to, or after these data are gathered from the community.

Many consultants consider these board discussions key to the search and selection process because they will help define and specify where the board wishes to see the district go and what the new superintendent's foci should be. Some consultants pride themselves on the amount of time and effort devoted to grappling with these difficult issues and may distinguish their services from others' by emphasizing how they help in this board development and visioning process. Various forms of situational analyses, goal setting, and prioritizing activities are often involved.

Some consultants lament that some boards either resist participating in, or choose not to devote the time necessary for, this preliminary work. Boards may prefer, instead, to move directly into identifying the qualities and background they desire in their new superintendent. A minority of consultants likewise prefer to move quickly to the latter because that will enable them to begin sooner the tasks of advertising and, in most cases, recruiting for the position. Ultimately, consultants discuss with board members a number of specific questions regarding the individual to be hired. These questions probe board preferences and relative rankings regarding ideal candidates' major field of study; degrees earned; prior experience in teaching and administration; longevity and grade levels of that experience; background in specific leadership positions, such as principal, assistant superintendent, or superintendent; prior district type(s) (rural, suburban, city) and size(s); location of prior district(s) (i.e., within- or out-of-state); relative strengths in business management versus curriculum and instruction; and skills in particular areas, such as collective negotiations, public relations, personnel management, facilities and construction, public speaking, politics, human relations, technology, and supervision.

Identification of candidate qualifications. All of this initial groundwork serves as a precursor to developing a profile of the hoped-for successor superintendent. This profile guides the phrasing of the documents and brochures designed for advertising the vacancy.

On one level, these brochures serve the purpose of acquainting prospective applicants with the job opening and the district. They include information about application procedures, deadlines, anticipated time frames for the selection process, salary range, fringe benefits, starting date, and equal employment opportunity policies. Details related to size are often mentioned: student enrollment, number of buildings and staff, square miles encompassed by the district, and sometimes even the number of school buses. Selected information about instructional programs, curricular or building initiatives, graduates, and district finances are also included. Sometimes, school board members' names, number of years served on the board, and the dates that their terms expire are listed. And there is almost always a section on the local community and geographic area, usually attempting to make the district sound as attractive as possible.

On a more substantive level, most such brochures follow the convention of identifying 6 to 12 descriptors of the essential qualities, characteristics, competencies, or experiences required and preferred of viable candidates. According to most consultants in this study, these descriptors are the criteria that will help guide the paper screening of applications and interview foci later in the process. However, Johnson's (1996) research concluded that "no single candidate can possibly embody all the skills, strengths, and traits sought by school districts. . . . [Such descriptions] reflect the combined wish lists of an array of constituents with varied preferences and priorities" (p. 31). Grogan's (1996) research proffers similar conclusions.

In this study, I reviewed scores of superintendency vacancy brochures and likewise found extraordinary combinations of expectations, often bordering on the heroic or saintly. The descriptors framed around abilities, skills, and practice tend to be broad and general, often incorporating the vocabulary of the current educational reform movement; for example, shared decision making, high academic standards, leadership vision, student-centeredness, focus on excellence, school-community partnerships, accountability, strategic planning, and community involvement. Sometimes, specific expertise in program development, business management, or another technical area is included. Along with these preferences for what the applicant has done or can do are references to desired personal traits, attitudes, attributes, or other affective characteristics. Frequently recurring words among these qualifiers are courage, integrity, flexibility, resourcefulness, and openness; as well as adjectives such as sensitive, responsive, accessible, ethical, energetic, dedicated, organized, sincere, innovative, knowledgeable, and inventive. As a board member explains, "Yes, all of those things will be listed in the brochure. And, in the beginning, we even thought we would find someone who met all those descriptions. But you learn that no one is going to have it all. When it comes down to seeing the real people, then you decide about giving up something here to get something there. It's how the board thinks about its priorities among those qualifications and when they actually see the person." (How the in-district interviews mediate the qualifying criteria will be discussed later in the book.)

Even with such broad lists of qualifiers, it is impossible for these brochures or profiles to capture the entirety of the consultant's discussions of priorities with the board or everything the board is actually looking for in the new hire. For most candidates, consultants, and board members, what's "between the lines" is as important as the written descriptors in vacancy advertisements. Consultants keep additional notes of their knowledge about the district and the board's unwritten selection criteria. A headhunter explains, "Some of the things boards raise we have to say to them, 'You know, if you start trying to write this down in an ad, it either isn't going to come across very well, or it's too complicated. So when we do the paper screening, we can look for those things. And we'll put those things on our list for when we do the interviews.'"

Board members confirm that, sometimes, criteria are included in published search documents to satisfy particular constituencies rather than to reflect the board's real interests or priorities. For example: "We happened to have a very strong School Business Official. So the board knew the new superintendent would have to understand budget and finance, but not be expert in it. But we still gave that qualification equal prominence in our brochure, so the community would know we were paying attention to their taxes." A board member from another district put it more bluntly: "Forget all the generalities that appear in the brochures. That's all a big P.R. thing. But the board knows what it needs, and if the consultant is worth his salt, he's in tune with them." A consultant corroborates that "you learn what's important to that board. What they mean by what's on the paper. It's sort of the hidden criteria." Another headhunter provides a more specific illustration: "One of the traits they were seeking was 'professionalism.' And what the board meant by that was they didn't want anyone going out in the community for drinks at all."

Other board members reveal how written specifications of qualifications are sometimes used to promote or preclude the candidacy of experienced administrators from within the district. A 12-year veteran board member's comments illustrate how this works: "What do you do with insiders who may want to apply? Do you set up the qualifications in such a way that they *can't* apply if you don't want them to? That's easy to do, by requiring a doctorate or certain specific kinds of previous experience. Or do you want to encourage them? Are you grooming anybody? That all has to be decided before you advertise."

Besides these examples of advertised criteria reflecting considerations other than the desired qualifications of the new superintendent, this research also surfaced illustrations of how consultants intentionally digress from the agreed-upon profiles in their screening of candidates to recommend to the board. A headhunter recounts, "I knew the board wanted someone with prior experience as a superintendent. But I also had to use my own judgment. There was an outstanding applicant who didn't meet that criterion but whom I felt the board would really take to if I could only get him in front of them. So I used that flexibility. And they ended up hiring him over two sitting superintendents."

Although there are ample opportunities to ignore stated selection criteria, there is also evidence that headhunters *introduce* their own qualifying (and disqualifying) criteria into the screening process (Kamler, 1995; Magowan, 1979). In this study, the following illustration demonstrates how idiosyncratic this can be. "We asked for a writing sample of all candidates. And I believe both substance and presentation are important. Some applicants typed it out on a piece of computer paper. Now when there were any mistakes in that, they had a problem with me. Because if there were mistakes there, it's because they were sloppy. Other people wrote it out longhand. When it's in their own handwriting, I'm less aggressive about a forgotten 'e' on something. Now the ones who I graded the highest were those who included both their handwritten draft, so that I know they could write, and their computer version, so I could get a sense of their productivity. So I use all of those kinds of things to help sort applicants." (By the way, there were no instructions to applicants about whether the writing sample should be typed, handwritten, or both.)

In a nutshell, then, a set of preferred candidate qualifications is identified by the hiring board and school community. Some are written (often in glowing, broad, and hyperbolic terms) and published through job advertisement. Some are unwritten and come to be understood through a series of private conversations between board members and the consultant.

Your application. It's common practice to require superintendent candidates to complete a district-specific application, in addition to providing a resumé, cover letter, and placement file of references. Consultants often provide school boards with sample forms that can be modified or adopted in their entirety. These application forms serve three purposes: (a) standardization of information provided in written form by the candidate, (b) reinforcement of high-priority interests of the district, and (c) augmentation of resumé data.

The forms often request quantification of candidate background data, such as present salary; annual budget and student enrollment in current district; the number of people reporting to the candidate; and listings of prior experience in terms of position titles, name and size of organization, and dates served in each prior role. Some applications also require considerable qualitative information, such as written essays on professional goals or educational philosophy, or responses to as many as a half-dozen specific questions that are so important to a particular district that their content can eliminate the candidate from further consideration. Such questions often relate to pressing challenges that the district faces—a financial dilemma, a community relations crisis, or the need to revise certain programs or curricula to comply with state requirements. A few applications also request copies of prior personnel evaluations of, and/or conducted by, the applicant. As explained by a consultant who strongly advocates the latter, "Personnel evaluations can be very revealing. They give you a strong sense of how the applicants view evaluation, whether or not they take it seriously and as an important part of the process of improvement and accountability."

As with personal interviews, a major rationale driving application requests for supplementary quantitative and qualitative data is the widespread perception that resumés and college transcripts "don't look all that different."

Summary and Implications

To this point, there's been a flurry of activity on the part of the board and consultant to prepare for the superintendent search. The flurry culminates in the identification of a profile of preferred candidate qualifications, including both public and privately understood selection variables. These written and unwritten criteria are variously used, neglected, and reinterpreted at different points in the process by boards and headhunters alike. So, what's a prospective applicant to do?

First, use your own informal networks of friends and colleagues to obtain additional information on what the district is really looking for in its next superintendent, regardless of what the published advertisement calls for. Also, don't be discouraged by what may appear to be "walk-on-water" criteria for selection; almost all superintendent vacancy brochures ask for more than any mere mortal can deliver.

Second, pay attention to the district's choices about whom it has involved in the needs identification phase of the process. These may provide important clues to a board's general approach to community involvement and shared decision making. Your own vision of stakeholder participation may be compatible, or dissonant, with this board's modus operandi. You'll want to know that early on.

Initial Preparation

- Set time lines and salary for search
- Review needs and goals of district
- Develop profile of qualifications
- Decide on community involvement
- Design brochure for dissemination

Advertisement and Recruitment

- Inform public and post vacancy
- Disseminate announcements and brochures
- Solicit nominations and recruit
- Accumulate applications

Initial Screen by Consultant

- Review of paper by individual/team
- Check references and do phone investigations
- Interview selected applicants
- Narrow to 10 to 12 candidates to promote to school board

Narrowing the Field of Candidates

- Profile 10 to 12 candidates for the board
- Discuss fit with board
- Narrow to five to six candidates for first round of in-district interviews

Preparation for In-District Interviews of Semifinalists

- Develop interview protocols
- Train in interviewing processes
- Decide on schedules, format, structure

Selection of Finalists

- Complete first round of interviews
- Receive advice from community committees
- Narrow to 2 to 3 finalists
- Complete second round of interviews by board

Hiring

- Visit finalist's district
- Finalize and sign contract
- Announce appointment to public

Figure 1.1: Overview of Board Search and Selection Processes

Third, understand that these preliminary preparations take time. Know that the apparent delay in advertising the opening is not intended to increase your anxiety as you await the opportunity to apply.

Finally, if you do turn out to be hired for the position, tap the wealth of community input and survey results that may have gone into the district "pulse-taking" described earlier. Either the consultant or the board will have kept summaries. This information about perceptions of district strengths, weaknesses, and desired future directions can be used to corroborate the results of your independent data gathering and, perhaps, test your own judgment of what's needed. You'll want to capitalize on any credible information already collected to help guide your start-up year.

2

What Is Recruiting and Interviewing Candidates All About?

Peter Calabrese, high school principal, finishes a game of racquetball and bumps into a neighboring district's superintendent in the locker room. After chatting about their respective matches that day, the superintendent offers to set up a meeting between Peter and his college roommate, a retired county superintendent now running a search for the Fredericksburg school board. Peter is happy in his current job and hadn't considered seeking another position. Although a superintendency was the last thing on his mind, before he knew it, Peter had met with the search consultant and been advanced as a semifinalist for an interview with the school board. He rushed to get an updated resumé and application paperwork filed before the board interview, as he had progressed that far in the process without having completed either.

Paul Healy, assistant superintendent in Willetts School District, has spent every Saturday morning for the past 4 months on the Internet, scrutinizing listings of superintendent position vacancy announcements from state education departments, administrators' professional organizations, school board associations, metropolitan newspaper classifieds, and university placement offices. He's devoted countless hours to updating and refining his placement file, customizing cover letters of interest, and writing thoughtful essays in response to required questions on application forms. Although Paul has submitted 16 completed applications, participated in telephone interviews with five different headhunters, and enjoyed the enthusiastic support of his current superintendent, his candidacy has never advanced to a hiring school board.

Why is Peter now a superintendent and Paul still looking? How do school board members and consultants think about the recruitment and advancement of applicants? What are some common practices that are invisible to you as a candidate? What kinds of interview questions can you anticipate? Why are informal networks so heavily relied upon in the process of superintendent search and selection? These are the questions this chapter will answer.

Eliciting Applicants

First, you need to know that school boards and search consultants are often ambivalent about recruitment. On one hand, board members voice suspicion of headhunters reputed to have an existing repertoire of favorite candidates whom they are trying to place. The latter are often referred to derogatorily as a "stable." On the other hand, boards often expect aggressive and extensive pursuit of the best possible slate of candidates for their consideration: "After all, that's what we hire them [the consultants] for!"

There appears to be less, but still some, ambivalence on the part of candidates in this study. Their discussions of recruitment center on instances in which they had received a call from a consultant (or a local superintendent or professor known to be well acquainted with the consultant), encouraging them to apply for a particular opening. For the most part, these calls are welcome, flattering, and self-validating for prospective applicants. But for some women and people of color, such recruitment raises concerns about possible tokenism: Is this genuine interest or window dressing for the sake of appearance? Is the consultant seeking a woman or racial/ethnic minority group member just to avoid a politically incorrect all-white male slate of semifinalists?

Consultants' perspectives also vary considerably. Many, whether regionally or nationally focused, consider recruitment the cornerstone of their services to boards. They are proud of their informal networks of contacts and candidate sources, market these connections as strengths, and view their major task as drawing upon those resources to produce a high-quality slate of candidates from which a board may make its selection. These consultants call prospective

candidates directly ("Are you interested in making a move?") or solicit names from their networks ("Whom do you know in your area
who is ready for a new challenge?"). Several of these consultants develop specialized niches of expertise and connection, such as the recruitment of candidates who are African American, candidates with
experience in urban districts, or candidates who have experience in
high-status suburban districts.

Other consultants do not recruit or solicit candidates at all. Instead, they interpret their role as facilitating a formal process of advertisement and screening of whichever applicants learn of the opening and choose to apply on their own. For some consultants, this is a
way of simplifying their task. For others, it is more purposeful: They
see this approach as a means of keeping the process strictly above
board, equally open to all, clean, rational, and professional.

One variation of the nonsolicitation approach is actually a kind
of passive (rather than active) recruitment. A headhunter explains
the distinction: "We will not go out to someone and say, 'Gee, you'd
be a great candidate in this district.' Now that's not to say some people will say to us, if they're in one of our searches and don't get the
job, 'Now you know what kind of district I'm interested in.' What we
will do in those cases is just send them the information when it's
ready. But that's different from going out and saying to somebody,
'Gee, we really think you'd be a great candidate.'"

Another nonrecruitment variation applies to a small number of
particular superintendent vacancies where, because the situation is
widely perceived as so desirable and applicants are so numerous,
consultants' pursuit of candidates is simply not needed.

Between these two ends of the continuum (i.e., aggressive to
nonexistent) are consultants who voice varying degrees of concern
about the practice of candidate recruitment. For some, the historical
vestiges of stables of protégés are a reputation they wish to avoid at
all costs: Boards won't hire them and candidates won't trust them, if
this were the case. Others are uncomfortable with how the word "recruitment" can be interpreted if they admit to practicing it: "I don't
mean stealing good people from other school boards." Or, "It's not
that I participate in the old good-ol'-boys system."

In practice, of course, even when consultants themselves do not
solicit or encourage particular applicants, there is always active recruitment taking place around any superintendency vacancy. Candi-

dates' experiences reveal that school board members, parents, teachers, county superintendents, school administrators, and others who have a direct or indirect interest in the new hire make the opening known and encourage favored acquaintances to submit applications. Like Peter, in the vignette that began this chapter, many candidates indicate that they would not have applied for a particular position had they not been encouraged informally to do so. Moreover, this encouragement often occurs before the vacancy is announced publicly or advertised: "The current superintendent is leaving, and I think you'd be perfect for the job." As a school board member explains, "I silently recruit, especially where I can encourage some diversity in the pool." In this instance, she was referring to race and gender.

Implications. What do these varying perspectives on recruitment mean for you as a potential future applicant? First, if you are encouraged to apply, understand that it's simply an invitation to be part of a pool of candidates, not an assurance that you'll be offered the job. It's important to keep your expectations realistic.

Second, be discreet—better yet, close-mouthed—about sharing how you came to be an applicant for the position, if you are, in fact, invited to apply. Given the apparent ambivalence about recruitment among boards and consultants, it will be unwise to flaunt any special connections or nominations made on your behalf. Today, virtually all position vacancy notices include official pronouncements of commitment to equal opportunity employment practices. Any intimations that partiality has been a factor in your candidacy may expose that pronouncement as untrue.

Paper Screening

The word is out, some recruitment has occurred, and applications have started to come in. What happens now behind the scenes?

Typically, the consultant receives the completed application forms, cover letters, resumés, and placement files. Several variations of this initial paper screening are practiced. For example, some headhunters work by themselves, evaluating each candidate's file against the district's criteria for the position—and their own interpretations of same. Some have assistants or others on their teams evaluate applications as a check on their own judgments. Some consultants partner with experienced school board members (not from the hiring district) or with retired superintendents to review applications. Some put together three- or four-person teams, from their own firms or elsewhere, to independently rank applicants and then deliberate rankings as a group. And some intentionally structure such teams to include gender and ethnic/racial diversity.

The proverbial bottom line is, you will probably never know exactly how your application was screened out, or in, before even having a chance to reach the school board or within-district selection committee. That's why search consultants are often referred to as gatekeepers in this process (Chase & Bell, 1990, 1994; Kamler, 1995).

In any case, some type of chart or spreadsheet is typically created, enabling the headhunter to provide snapshot summaries to the school board. Sometimes, variables are keyed to specific descriptors that appeared in position vacancy advertisements. These summaries often compare years of experience, size of schools or districts of prior experience, administrative positions held currently and previously, and number of years in various positions.

Some consultants send the board weekly updates of these summaries as additional applications come in. Others wait until the deadline date for all applications, then present the board with one summary. This is a time in the process when board members and candidates may feel like nothing is happening, as they await word on the status of applications.

In contrast, for the consultants, it's a very busy period. If the applicant pool looks thin, they may engage in their most aggressive kinds of recruitment. Besides reviewing paper and recruiting, they are simultaneously conducting reference checks, usually by phone and usually only on the applicants they consider "keepers" (that is, those deemed best qualified as a result of the paper screening). The reference checks help headhunters determine which of the applicants they wish to interview personally. Both the reference checking and personal interviews help the consultant narrow the pool. Many consultants interview between 12 and 15 applicants, with the goal of bringing 10 to 12 names (or files) to the board for closer review. But again, there exist considerable variations here. Some consultants interview more or fewer candidates, some aim to bring more or fewer to the board for closer review, and some receive so few applications that they're trying to expand rather than narrow the field.

Reference checking. As in recruitment, an interrelated network of informal contacts is used to gain additional insights about applicants. Many consultants check with other superintendents in the candidate's area of current employment or local educational administration professors: "What do you hear about John or Jane Doe?" As a courtesy, they may phone the references listed on the candidate's resumé, but often, because those are expected to be positive, they are not given much weight. Those contacts may, however, provide leads to other people with knowledge of the individual's experiences, accomplishments, and history.

There are multiple purposes for these checks. One is to corroborate information provided by the applicant. A second is to provide a context, richness, and personality to the experiences and attributes delineated or written about by the candidate. A third and key purpose is to minimize risk to the hiring school district.

Do you remember the skeletons and blemishes on your professional record mentioned in Chapter 1? At this point, the consultant is trying to ascertain what's really in your closet, to get a more complete understanding of any skeletons, and to learn of anything that might be interpreted as a fatal flaw by a school board or community. These may include a past incident of sexual harassment; a driving-while-intoxicated conviction; a habit of treating board members with disrespect; a buy-out of a previous contract; or a termination of employment, to name just a few.

Here's where the real digging occurs. The inquiries about strengths, weaknesses, accomplishments, and shortcomings provide background information. Some of the most powerful responses are to questions such as, "Based on what you know about this person and what I've told you about the vacancy, would you bring this person to the board for an interview?" "Would you hire Jane/John for this job, knowing what you know about her or him?" If from a trusted source or from more than one source, negative answers to these kinds of questions will usually eliminate you from further consideration. According to a veteran headhunter, "Toward the end of the conversation with a reference, you always try to bring it down to a yes or no kind of thing."

According to other consultants and candidates, however, it is not only the "no's" that are harmful to advancement in the process, but also the "maybe's," the passivity about promoting a candidate, and the silences. A headhunter makes this observation about the regional superintendents relied upon as references in some states: "I don't know any one of them who will go out of his or her way to *un-*promote somebody. But some don't promote hard enough. It makes a difference if they wait to be called or initiate the call themselves. For example, anytime you contacted [superintendent] about [candidate], he was effusive because he knew how good she was. But what would have been better for that candidate is if he had been out, on her behalf, talking to people and saying, 'I've got an administrator you really ought to take a look at for that search.'" Many candidates echoed this view: "If [my superintendent] was called by someone, I'm sure he'd give a positive recommendation. But a lot of times, it's helpful for them to initiate the call, to trigger you into the system. Because otherwise, your application can get overlooked."

More implications. Taken together, these examples underscore the importance of the webs of informal connections among incumbent administrators, headhunters, and school boards. They also illustrate how great the overlap is between recruitment and background checking in these networks of trusted referrals. Do you know who the key players are in your state and region? How much effort have you expended investigating which experienced superintendents' or university professors' opinions are most highly regarded among their peers? Who among them is best connected to the various search consultants in your part of the country? Who would be willing to introduce you to key referral sources and headhunters? How can you at least get a foot in the door to an interview with some consultants?

Consultant Interviewing

Most consultants speak directly with any applicants whom they intend to promote to the board as among the 10 to 12 best matches for the advertised criteria. If geographic distance is great, this conversation may occur by telephone. Often, it's done in person. Frequently, it's brief. Essentially, consultants want to have some firsthand knowledge of your communication skills. They want to minimize the risk of forwarding to a board or community a candidate who doesn't appear to fit the bill. Some headhunters see these interviews as recruitment opportunities for future openings: after all, only one of these people will be hired. The rest may appear as applicants in subsequent searches for other boards. Ongoing relationships can be established here . . . by you and by the consultant.

For the candidates in this study, this preliminary interview is viewed as a key gate to traverse. Perceptions of the consultant's fairness and professionalism get formed by candidates here. At their most negative, these interviews can involve long treks across the state (or region) for 15-minute encounters with little substantive discussion. They are sometimes viewed by candidates as "pilgrimages" to "kiss the ring" of the gatekeeper, where the most appropriate behavior seems to be to express gratitude and humility. These preliminary meetings are sometimes perceived as inconvenient and time-consuming rituals for very busy administrators, especially in those cases where candidates have spoken with the consultant several times before in their professional career. And, as mentioned in the earlier discussion of recruitment, some candidates wonder whether the interview is genuine or gender or racially motivated.

One consultant in this study is notably distinct in his practices in these regards. He does not conduct private preliminary interviews with applicants. He avoids this practice for four reasons. First, he interprets his role as facilitator of applicants to the board and eschews the role of barrier, weeder, or gatekeeper. Second, he considers information gathering through off-the-record telephone reference checking a better use of time than one-on-one interaction with candidates. Third, he believes it more informative to watch the candidate in a group interview with the board: "I think it's beneficial to watch people interview with a whole group rather than one person. It's very easy to play one person; very different when you're in a group interview situation." Fourth, overall, he minimizes the value of interviewing as a significant criterion for determining quality of prospective superintendents.

This latter point is especially interesting, given the strong influence that interviews wield in most other superintendent search practices. (More on this later.) The following captures his reasoning behind this point:

> If somebody has got an outstanding record as an educator, then why should we let just one skill—interviewing—eliminate them from advancement? . . . Are we saying that one of the skills that a person has to have as a superintendent is to be able to interview?

I would say, no. I don't see where that's a match in terms of the actual requirements of the job. Now, you certainly have to be able to present to the public. And I think we find those things out when the finalists go through a day-long activity at the end where they meet all the community groups and the staff. We find out, Can they present a leadership image? But I'm not sure that, as superintendent, they ever again interview for the job. . . . That's kind of like the teacher evaluation that's only based on a 45-minute classroom observation, versus evaluation of their total performance. I spend a lot of time talking to people who are behind the scenes, who know what kind of a person that person really is. For example, How do they react to stress? I don't find a lot of that out in an interview. You have to find it out by talking to people. And by talking to enough people, you begin to get a picture of who is this candidate.

This rationale captures the apparent disconnect between the abilities required of competent leadership as a superintendent and the skills required of interviewing. Embedded in the rationale is the belief that information about past performance over time is a better predictor of future success in the superintendency than are the solo performances of candidates in time-limited interview situations. Also embedded here is faith that the diligent pursuit of multiple data sources will produce a trustworthy representation of the applicant. Coupled with the previous points on reference checking, all of this increases the importance of headhunters'—and your—networks of contacts and informants.

Narrowing the Field of Candidates

So far, the consultant holds pretty much all the cards. He or she has seen all of the applications for the position; has completed, or overseen the completion of, the paper screening; has talked with lots of people about the applicants who seem the strongest (or who have the most potential) on paper; has personally interviewed those candidates judged to be the best matches for a particular school district (notwithstanding the individual just described as an exception); and has compiled summary information for the school board.

All of this has taken anywhere between 2 and 6 weeks. Candidates are wondering what is happening with their applications. The board is anxious to get a peek at some real people.

Most consultants offer to let the board see any or all applicant files. Very few board members take them up on the invitation. Failure to make the offer, however, seems to prompt increased interest in the files by board members. To wit, "We were wondering what were the resumés like that the headhunter didn't consider. So we asked to see them, and one board member spent a whole afternoon looking through all the files on behalf of the board."

At this point, a lengthy meeting occurs between the consultant and board. The headhunter usually provides a quick overview of the numbers and, perhaps, demographics of the total pool of applicants. (Do you remember the charts and spreadsheets mentioned earlier?) He or she reminds the board of the criteria and descriptors upon which they had agreed at the start of the search. The consultant identifies the 10 to 12 applicants who best meet those criteria, usually providing a 10- to 15-minute verbal summary of each, including feedback from reference checks. After hearing this information, the board typically reviews the 10 to 12 files, discusses, deliberates, and chooses the five or six candidates they believe to be the strongest of that group. These become the slate of semifinalists that will participate in the first round of in-district interviews by the school board and, sometimes, other community groups.

Again, an interesting outlier example in this study distinguished itself from the more common pattern just described. Some consultants employ a process that involves a non-school board committee whose charge is to interview the 10 to 12 top candidates (from the consultant's and board's paper screening) and narrow that field to three finalists. The interview committee consists of about a dozen people, representing students, parents, teachers, administrators, staff, and community residents.

Although the composition of this committee is not unusual, this practice is distinct in several ways. First, more candidates participate in in-district interviews than is normally the case; 10 or 12, rather than five or six. Second, a nonboard community group plays a more significant role than is typical, because this interview team has the power to determine the three-person slate of candidates to be seen by the board. And third, the school board interviews the finalists once, rather than twice.

In these consultants' views, the more common practices of bringing in five to six candidates for in-district interviews, and having the
board and any community groups interview simultaneously, contribute to the perception of community participation as "window
dressing" rather than "a real screening function." Other consultants
with whom I shared this example were appalled at "how much control the board gives away" via this approach. The point is, you may
encounter various forms of interviewing and combinations of players as you advance through the early stages of screening on your way
to the school board.

Preparation for In-District Interviews

Frequently, the consultant (or his or her designee) provides
training for both the board and any nonboard groups who participate in candidate interviews. One piece of this training focuses on le-
galities and compliance with regulations governing fair employment
practices. Consultants identify inquiries that are unlawful to make in
an employment interview situation (e.g., How old are you? Have you
ever been arrested? Are you planning to have children? Were you
born in the United States?). They give examples of statements about
the community or organization to avoid (e.g., This is a Protestant
school district).

Again, logistical concerns are addressed: when and where the interviews will occur, if or how the consultant will participate, how the
candidates will be kept from bumping into one another as they enter
and exit the interview site, what forms will be used to record responses, and what rating systems should be followed.

Questions to anticipate. Another piece of this training centers on
the questions to be asked of interviewees. Often, consultants provide
lists of possible queries. The sample lists examined for this study
were often divided into seven or eight categories of questions, including the general topics of superintendent-school board working
relationships, communications, staff development, budgeting and
business functions, collective bargaining, curriculum and instructional programs, personnel evaluation, and facilities. Sometimes, inquiries are geared to eliciting specific examples relevant to the category from the interviewee's previous experiences, such as, "What
experiences have you had in financing bus purchases?" or "Please

explain the budget-making process you use or with which you are familiar in your present district." Sometimes, questions are focused more specifically on the hiring district's current situation: "How will you judge if we have good programs in math, language arts, science, and social studies?" In addition, reactions to likely "critical incidents" (Berman, 1997) are often sought: "If we needed to dismiss a tenured teacher, what would you recommend as the procedures to be followed?" Some questions are geared to broad generalities or philosophy: "What are your thoughts on mainstreaming and inclusion of students with special needs?" or "What would you say are some key principles for maintaining an effective relationship between the superintendent and the school board?" And there is often a category called "other" or "personal" that encompasses questions like "What are your long-term professional goals?"

Boards may select from these lists, adapt them, or invent new questions of their own. Some consultants advise that questions be limited to, or focused on, the criteria originally specified for the search. Sometimes, new needs or interests emerge in the district that are quite distinct from the profile developed at the start of the process. These might include, for example, the unexpected exit of the district's assistant superintendent for curriculum or an unanticipated budget deficit.

In many cases, a set of common questions to be asked of each candidate is compiled, and systems for rating responses and/or providing feedback are agreed upon. Sometimes, the sequence of questions or topics will be predetermined, or perhaps particular board members will agree to raise certain questions.

Another, less conventional format for conducting interviews is explained by this consultant: "I worked with one board who didn't want to just sit around and ask questions round-robin style. So they decided to develop a list of 12 issues. And when the candidate came in, they handed the person the list, told them they had three or four minutes to look it over, and then could just start talking about the issues, in any order. What the board was looking for was where candidates would start, and how they related the issues to one another and combined them. The board actually did end up asking follow-up questions to what the candidates said, but the questions came out more naturally."

Interviewing. There is inevitably some tension between the benefits of a consistently structured interview process and the desire to create a comfortable and open atmosphere for the interviewees and candidate. Consultants advise boards and interview committees of the desirability of eliciting sufficient information, as well as pursuing generally the same substantive areas with each candidate, for both consistency and comparative purposes. This parallels advice found in references on standards for general personnel selection practices (Castallo, Fletcher, Rosetti, & Sekowski, 1991; Castetter, 1996; Rebore, 1991).

However, rote reading of questions and rigid, preordained turn taking often preclude the development of engaging and revealing conversations. The goal is often to achieve some balance between standardization and fluidity. This usually results in what could be termed semistructured interviewing. As illustrated by this consultant, "One of the key things is that you ask at least four or five basic questions of *all* candidates. If you don't do that, you don't have the ability to compare the candidates. So we allow school board members to get off on some tangents, but at some point they have to ask the same five to six basic questions."

Despite efforts to train interviewers, digressions and lack of uniformity among interviews are not uncommon. For example, a 14-year veteran school board member who had participated in the hiring of three different superintendents explains: "We were always given a list of things we could not ask. And lots of times we were each given a question. But we didn't usually stick to those too much. Sometimes, after interviewing the first candidate, there would be something that you pick up on that you want to pursue with the second candidate. So, then, you may ask some different questions with a second or third candidate."

Consultants may sit in on the interviews with the board/community, occasionally as group facilitators but more often as observers. Sometimes, their purpose is to monitor the process and keep the interview on track so that excessive inconsistencies or digressions do not occur. Another purpose is for the headhunter to become better informed about the individual's background knowledge and communication skills in groups. Again, the unsuccessful candidates in one district may appear in future searches, so this is a means of further expanding consultants' informal networks of potential recruits.

Although most superintendent candidate interviews are conducted in person, there is also some evidence that technology is changing conventional practices. Several consultants and candidates provided examples of using interactive video conferencing to enable boards to avoid the expense of transporting distant candidates to the first round of interviews. The candidates went to studio facilities at a nearby school, university, or commercial photocopying site to participate. Also, in a few instances, television stations conducted half-hour interviews with each of the semifinalist candidates and broadcast them over local cable television. In the words of the consultant assisting the board in one of those searches, "So, you could stay home, eat popcorn, drink a beer, and watch the interview on cable."

Selection of Finalists

Sometimes, the top two or three candidates (from the typical five or six semifinalists) bubble to the top quickly for the board. Occasionally, board agreement is reached through unstructured discussion, with the consultant, at this point, intentionally limiting his or her influence on the substance (though perhaps not the format) of the conversations. At times, board norms for consensus seeking prevail, allowing each member an opportunity to be heard prior to more free-wheeling discussion and decision making. Other times, the consultant may take the lead in structuring the process in some more formal way, such as by having board members write down (anonymously) their rankings of the semifinalists (i.e., first, second, and third choice) without discussion, and then tallying and displaying results for the whole group and facilitating the discussion of relative strengths and weaknesses of the candidates. Regardless of the process employed, eventually, the field of five or six semifinalists is narrowed to two or three.

Whereas in the first round of in-district interviews, candidates may have spent an hour or two being questioned, the second and final round (for these two to three people) is typically a full-day process. At this point, virtually all boards choose to involve groups other than themselves. The candidate often moves from a meeting with a parent group, to another with a group of teacher representatives, to another with administrators, to another with some students, and so on. This visit usually includes a tour of the district. Sometimes, a community forum is scheduled, where anyone from the educational system or community can attend, observe, and ask questions of the candidate. For the candidate, stamina is of the essence. The day typically culminates with a dinner session with the school board, including the candidate's spouse.

Some boards include additional tasks for the semifinalists beyond the multiple interviews, forums, and dinner. For example, one district attempted to simulate a real-life, unanticipated, "in-basket" problem for each of the three semifinalist candidates to address by taking 45 minutes to compose a letter of response. As one of the hiring board members saw it, "We learned a lot from that. It had to do with how collegial the person's approach was and what the tone of the letter was. Also, the superintendent does have to work under pressure and write letters quickly sometimes."

That same district also required a more planned simulation. Five days before the full-day interview, the board notified the three semifinalists that they would need to make a presentation to the board, as if at a regular board meeting. They could use whatever means they wished, including overhead transparencies or computer-generated slides. Here, the board was looking for communication skills, dealing with constrained time parameters, and substance. In one board member's words: "We gave them a time limit. And with one finalist, it was a lot of sizzle and no steak. He didn't get the job." But again, these two illustrations are more the exception than the norm in narrowing the field of semifinalists. More commonly, board and multiple stakeholder group interviews are relied upon.

Usually, when groups other than the board participate in the interviews, they are charged with the task of identifying strengths and weaknesses of each candidate. They are instructed to refrain from ranking the candidates (i.e., this is our top choice, our second favorite). They are reminded that their input is advisory to the board, and that this should not be confused with decision-making authority. Informants for this research report that these groups often find clever ways to circumvent many of these directives. Both school board members and consultants confirm that, regardless of the quality of training provided, the efforts to design feedback forms that narrowly define evaluation parameters, or the passion with which these groups' roles are defined and delimited, most stakeholder groups "let us know who their top choice is, who they find unacceptable, and what they want to see us do!"

Perhaps not surprisingly, deciding upon the one top candidate among the final two or three is usually much more difficult for the board than the earlier processes of elimination to narrow the slate. Why is this so? Often, all three remaining candidates are quite strong administrators. However, their strengths may be in distinct areas, and, of course, each candidate will also have some weaknesses. So, in part, this stage of decision making involves revisiting the qualifications criteria identified at the start of the search and attempting to objectively assess each finalist's strengths and weaknesses against those standards. But this is far from an exclusively rational exercise.

It is also, in part, a political process. By this point, the school board has received feedback on the final two or three candidates from a wide variety of stakeholder groups. When these various groups do not agree among themselves on relative strengths and weaknesses of the candidates, or when they each have a different favorite, the decision is complicated for the board. Even when the various groups do agree among themselves, if the board sees things differently, it is left in the uncomfortable position of choosing to hire a candidate not favored by any of its constituencies' representatives.

Besides the formalized political process of stakeholder group feedback from candidate interviews, some of these groups are also likely to have engaged their unique informal networks to gather additional information. That is, once the semifinalists' names are known, the administrator subgroup makes calls to other administrators who might know the candidates. The teachers' group makes similar calls to its colleagues. If candidates' names are leaked publicly, the media or other special interest groups (e.g., taxpayer organizations, religion- or race/ethnicity-based coalitions) may also initiate their own investigation into semifinalists' history, background, and reputation.

Some of the results of this digging will be communicated to individual board members behind the scenes (e.g., through phone calls to their homes or by buttonholing them in the local grocery store). When the media are involved, front page features in local newspapers may emerge, as well as local television coverage. Depending upon the nature of what is uncovered, additional community constituencies may become mobilized to exert their influence on the selection decision. These political pressures exacerbate the difficulty of the final selection for some school boards. When names and issues become public, candidates' lives are also directly affected, sometimes producing significant backlash. This point is elaborated more fully in the discussion of confidentiality in the next chapter.

Summary

The mix we have so far involves just two or three semifinalists, all of whom are very skilled but none of whom is outstanding in every area; solicited feedback from a half-dozen or so constituency groups, structured by the school board and mostly internal to the school district; unsolicited political pressures from any number of sources; a set of written qualifications used to advertise the vacancy months before; the personal judgments of probably five to nine school board members who have interviewed each of the semifinalists twice; and, often, an outside consultant facilitating and influencing the entire process. How does the school board sort through all of this sometimes conflicting information to identify its top choice? In a word, intuition.

Previous research on educational personnel selection underscores the dominance of face-to-face interviews in decision making and, within interviews, the predominance of numerous subjective factors (Castallo et al., 1991; Castetter, 1996). For example, Rebore (1991, p. 76) notes the prevalence of interviewers' hunches in selection decisions.

Other studies focused specifically on the superintendency provide evidence that "feel" and "visceral response" often become important in consultants' and school board selections (Kamler, 1995). Similarly, Rickabaugh (1986) found that appearance, manner of speech, and nonverbal behaviors were factors contributing to the subjectivity and high degree of influence of interviews in superintendent selection. Baltzell and Dentler's (1983) studies of school administrators' hiring found widespread reliance on "localistic notions of 'fit' or 'image'" (p. 7).

Time and again, this study's informants (whether consultants, board members, or candidates) confirmed that, in the end, the chemistry between school board members and interviewees is what matters most. What does this mean? Primarily, it means level of comfort and ease with one another on an interpersonal level. It's a matter of "with whom can I see myself working day in and day out" for the next several years? With whom is it easiest for me to communicate? "If I had to call someone in the middle of the weekend with an important concern, whom would I feel free to call?" "Whom can I see leading this district and grappling with the multiple pressures exerted on superintendents and boards?" Yes, each of the two or three candidates who remain for consideration is an experienced and qualified educational administrator. But with whom do I relate best? What does my "gut" tell me? I've seen the paperwork, I've heard others' opinions, but what's my own intuitive response to the candidates as people? (Stay tuned for more on the inappropriate biases that overreliance on "intuition" brings with it, in Part 2 of this volume.)

Implications. What are the implications of these realities for you? One is to be genuine. Because fuzzy phenomena like interpersonal chemistry and gut feelings are so influential to interviewers, there's no sense being anyone but yourself when you make it that far. You may connect; you may not.

As underscored in the "questions to anticipate" section of this chapter, some interview questions are predictable. Think about them beforehand, organize your thoughts with care, and rehearse. Of course, there will always be unanticipated queries. Don't waste energy lamenting an occasional stumble. Prepare for what you can, learn from the surprises, and view this as a long-term process of cultivating your communication skills.

Know in advance what you would like to share about your accomplishments, values, and appropriateness for the position. Where possible, incorporate these preplanned points in the interview, making clear links to the questions raised. Also, connect your responses to the stated criteria advertised for the position.

Clearly, search consultants can be a powerful part of superintendent selection. Be aware that even if your meetings with headhunters are framed as informal chats, they are screening interviews that hold great sway. Treat them as such.

If there are blemishes, gaps, or anything that can be construed as a skeleton in your professional or personal background, discuss them directly with the consultant in preliminary conversations. He or she will assuredly receive interpretations of these experiences from others. Make the opportunity to control the context and elaboration of details from your own perspective.

The advice offered above assumes that you make it to the face-to-face encounters with headhunters and school boards. This chapter also reveals salient practices related to recruitment, nominations, and prescreening. What can you do in those regards?

First, identify either the highest frequency consultants in your area or the headhunters who specialize in the type of district you intend to target in your own career (e.g., large urban districts; "light-house" suburban communities; small, up-and-coming school systems). Experienced superintendents in your state will be able to help you identify these individuals or firms and their specialties.

Then, be creative in thinking about ways to make your skills and accomplishments visible to these people. You might make a presentation at a meeting they're likely to attend, chair a committee for an organization in which they're likely to participate, or get your photo in a conference program they're likely to peruse. As a general rule, headhunters will be present where large numbers of incumbent superintendents and school board members are gathered. Check with state-level professional organizations for conference programs and locations.

I hope you've noticed that I'm not recommending buying lunch for consultants, calling them at home, or hovering around them at cocktail hours. Save the schmoozing for another time. At the preparation and recruitment stages, stick to the basics. Do good work. Earn a solid reputation. And take the initiative to ensure that your skills and accomplishments are visible beyond your immediate region. As the previous chapter illustrated, school boards hire headhunters based, at least in part, on their confidence in a particular consultant's knowledge of who's out there. By attending to these basics, you can become one of the "who's out there" known to key consultants and incumbent superintendents. This preliminary work is often essential to your moving beyond unsolicited applications and becoming one of the recruited and interviewed.

3

How Are Hiring and Powerbrokering Related?

G ail Solomon, superintendent for 6 years in the Dysar School District, hangs up the phone and collects her thoughts. She's delighted to learn that she is one of the Windhem school board's top two choices for its superintendency. Yet she dreads their upcoming visit. She'll have to drop what she's doing to attend to the hefty logistical tasks of arranging for a Windhem board delegation to meet with faculty, staff, parents, students, community members, and administrators in her current district. She knows she can expect immediate inquiries from the local newspaper and teachers' union, probing why she wants to leave the district. She anticipates the anxiety of faculty, principals, her own board members, and others concerned about the numerous projects pending in Dysar, and what her departure from the district may mean to them. Her new job pursuits will now become public knowledge, and she'll have a lot of explaining to do. All this, along with the Windhem visitation within the next 8 days, promises to create an extra-busy, stressful, and exciting time for Gail and her family.

In the meantime, Christopher Ritter, search consultant to the Windhem board, is tearing his hair out because Chandlet school board members could not come to agreement on any of the candidates he forwarded for interviewing and board consideration. He cannot believe that none of the five talented semifinalists was deemed acceptable. Dissensus on the Chandlet board seems insurmountable. Christopher's unsure if he'll ever get them to agree on anyone.

But then he gets an unexpected call from Larry Sandles, a retired superintendent serving as interim in Chandlet. Larry grew to like and respect a bright young business manager in the last district in which he had served as interim superintendent. Although Chandlet's vacancy advertisement emphasized the need for a curricular and instructional leader, Larry felt the board might connect with this young man. So, he went out, recruited the business manager at the eleventh hour, and brought him in to interview with the Chandlet school board. All but one board member pretty much fell in love with the eleventh-hour candidate. At Larry's urging, the board agrees to a unanimous public vote on the appointment. The former business manager is now Chandlet school superintendent.

What should you know about superintendent hiring and power-brokering behind the scenes? This chapter sheds light on how informal systems of connections influence access to the superintendency. It explores the ways that common consultant practices shape the perspectives of school board members. It analyzes how the power and influence of different players has changed over time with respect to identifying and employing school superintendents. It examines some of the most anxiety-producing issues for superintendent applicants: school board dissensus, confidentiality, communications during the search and selection process, the time it takes, visitations by the hiring board, and contract negotiations prior to appointment. And it relates all of these factors to you, the potential future candidate.

Let's start with some of Gail's issues, the applicant mentioned in the first vignette above.

Visitations

For some boards and consultants, it's common practice to have several board members visit the current school district of the tentative final candidate, prior to offering him or her the job. The purpose of such visits is usually confirmatory. In other words, it is an opportunity to corroborate firsthand the information gleaned previously from the candidate and the reference checks. It is a chance for some members of the hiring board to meet with representatives of key constituencies in the favored finalist's current work setting.

Most consultants work hard to dissuade boards from visiting any more than the top candidate's district. But this is a piece of the process that apparently has changed considerably in the past 10 to 15 years. Previously, it had been customary to visit the communities and schools of the two or three most highly regarded semifinalists

(Afton, 1985; Roberts, 1996). Currently, visitations are seldom used to compare and contrast findings from semifinalists' districts. Visitations are now widely viewed as disruptive and intrusive, since only one of the remaining candidates will actually be exiting his or her current district. Also, such travels are time-consuming and expensive for school boards. Hence, a second site visit is conducted only if something so disturbing is discovered in the first district that it necessitates elimination of the top candidate and reconsideration of the second most favored applicant.

It is interesting to note that the literature on quality personnel selection practices often recommends direct observation of candidates' skills whenever possible (Castetter, 1996; Rosse & Levin, 1997). Work sampling and firsthand observations of performance are considered solid means of enhancing the validity of information obtained in less direct ways.

However, the tradition of school board visitations to semifinalists' districts is rarely focused on observing candidates in action. Instead, they are more akin to additional reference checking, albeit in person.

Typically, the hiring board identifies the general roles of people with whom they would like to meet (e.g., PTA members, teacher union representatives), but it is left up to the candidate to attend to the logistics of orchestrating the visitation day. From candidates' perspectives, although this is a difficult and time-consuming task, they typically do get to hand-pick the individuals and groups with whom the visitors will meet formally. Naturally, it is impossible to prevent spontaneous or informal interactions that might occur during the visit.

A few boards are more prescriptive in their approach to the site visit. For example, they may limit the amount of leeway the candidate has in orchestrating exclusively positive interactions by requesting the inclusion of some likely "singletons." The latter may include the editor of the local newspaper or the youth officer for the high school. Also, the hiring board may insist on meeting with all, rather than just the candidate's self-selected, school board members.

In practice, these visits serve to reassure board members of their conclusions reached earlier and from afar. The visits also ensure that the candidate's interest in exiting his or her current position becomes public knowledge. Up to that time, the candidate may have shared his or her outside job pursuits only with selected confidants, the school board, or the board president. This raises the issues of confidentiality and communication in all parts of the search and selection process.

Confidentiality. There are several structural vehicles employed by the consultant facilitators that are aimed at guarding the privacy of applicants. For example, most incorporate direct instruction about confidentiality into their initial discussions with school boards and into their training sessions with the board and other community groups to be involved in candidate interviews. It is in these sessions that consultants discuss not only candidates' expectations of and needs for privacy, but also the potential negative consequences of breaches of confidentiality. Often cited are the possibilities that the wider public and media will obtain applicants' names and begin their political pressuring for (and against) candidates early in the process, that qualified applicants will remove themselves from consideration if they cannot trust the hiring board to be discreet about personnel matters, or that the consultant's recruitment efforts will be thwarted if prospective applicants believe that they will be subjected to public scrutiny prior to becoming a semifinalist for the position.

In addition to these direct educative initiatives, most consultants also structure the interview schedule so that as little time as possible passes between interviews. This serves at least two purposes. First, interviewers may more easily remember and calibrate their assessments of candidates if the candidates are viewed in close proximity to one another. Second, a tight schedule of interviews may minimize the opportunities for either leaks or undue external influences on board members' and other interviewers' judgments.

Communication. As mentioned earlier, there is a time when the consultant is busy receiving and reviewing applications, recruiting, and conducting reference checks and preliminary interviews while candidates and school boards wait for results of this prescreening. The school board members in this study expressed little concern about how they were kept apprised of developments during this phase of the process. Candidates, on the other hand, voiced several complaints.

Virtually all experienced consultants have routinized procedures for disseminating letters indicating receipt of applications and notifying applicants of missing paperwork. Beyond that, things become fuzzy. Some candidates are disappointed when they do not receive any word after their screening interview with the consultant. Successful applicants usually receive personal phone calls notifying them of their advancement to the semifinalist and finalist groups to be interviewed by the hiring district. Candidates considered clearly unqualified also tend to receive fairly prompt written notification. In other words, communication is often most clear with the "definitely recommend to the board" and the "definitely not" groups. You may find yourself in one of those categories.

However, because there is also typically a "maybe" group of applicants, and because consultants do not know whether their own sorting of the applicants will meet with the board's approval, there are almost always candidates who will be held (without their knowledge) in a "will possibly move forward" category. On one hand, consultants and boards feel the need to hedge their bets, keeping some next-best applications in abeyance in case their preferred candidates take positions elsewhere, withdraw their applications for other reasons, commit some unforgivable gaffe at the last minute, perform poorly in the interview, or have some negative performance history emerge late in the final reference checking.

What this means for you is that some highly qualified candidates receive very little communication about their status in the process. From some applicants' perspectives, it is both inconsiderate and unprofessional to be left waiting with such scant information. Although some consultants are forthright about this in-between status, the conventional wisdom seems to be that good candidates will withdraw themselves if they know they are considered the backup or second choice of the consultant or board. This limitedness of communication is seen as a necessary precaution by those doing the hiring but as an agonizing guessing game by some candidates. This uncertainty applies equally to the stages between consultant interview and first in-district interview, between being one of the five or six board interviewees and one of the two or three semifinalists, and between being one of the top two or three candidates and being the new hire. The end result is sometimes that very good candidates (such as yourself) will not have heard anything about their status until after the successful candidate has confirmed acceptance of the board's contract.

Whether essential or not to the selection process, some candidates interpret this limited communication as less than professional treatment by particular consultants. Some even avoid submitting subsequent applications when they know that that same consultant is assisting another board in its search for a superintendent.

The advice pertinent to prospective applicants is to try not to personalize such gaps in communication. They will inevitably occur. A better understanding of the nature of the selection process from consultants' and school boards' perspectives may help you appreciate these ebbs and flows in timing and information sharing.

Appointment

Previous research on school board norms reveals that, particularly for high-profile decisions, unanimity is always preferred to split votes (Cistone, 1982; First & Walberg, 1992; Tallerico, 1989; Zeigler & Jennings, 1974). This holds true for the appointment of the successful candidate to the superintendency. These norms are reflected in the following statement from a board handbook on superintendent selection: "Unanimous selection is good public policy. It gives promise of harmonious relationships between the school board and the superintendent and reinforces confidence in the board and superintendent" (NYSSBA, 1988, p. 11). Or, put more bluntly by one of the board members in this study, "If it's not public unanimously, you've already set the new person up for a lot of problems." What he meant was that particular interest groups can ascertain the limited board support of the superintendent and use that knowledge to more easily mobilize pressure for their preferred agendas.

Consistent with this theme of conflict containment, the specific provisions and terms of the superintendent's employment contract are important to both school boards and candidates. The negotiation of the written agreement can set the tone for subsequent board-superintendent relationships. It can also affect community relations, as "the contract between the parties will be a public document and should be negotiated with the expectation that it might be published in the local newspapers" (NYSSBA, 1995, p. 12). Many candidates and school boards avoid direct negotiation themselves and, instead, hire an attorney for this task. You should go this route, too, because it's usually worth the investment. Veteran superintendents and their state professional organizations can help you identify attorneys experienced in contract negotiations.

Some consultants take on this intermediary negotiating role themselves, and they market this feature as a part of their services to the board. A slight variation of this service is that, although not serving as intermediaries in contract negotiations, some search firms will conduct analyses of the board's current contract with the exiting superintendent. They examine the contract, comment on what is included and what is absent, corroborate how it comports with current education law and regulations, and note how it compares with other superintendent contracts.

Consultants also are accustomed to providing samples of press releases and otherwise assisting the board in making the formal announcement of its final selection after the contract has been signed. Often, the successful candidate is involved in the development and timing of the announcement, because there are so many important implications for his or her current district of employment. You should be prepared to attend to this important task. Actually, there's no reason why you couldn't have already drafted several possible versions of how you would like the news announced in your community—perhaps during one of those long waits alluded to earlier.

Time and timing. How long does all of this take, from the time a board knows its current superintendent will be exiting to the time a new superintendent is selected? It varies widely, but 4 to 6 months seems the minimum; a year, the maximum, under normal circumstances.

At the start of the process, most boards are anxious to get on with the business of conducting the search and therefore try to finalize the consultant selection decision expeditiously. Still, it may take weeks for the board to obtain consultants' search proposals, conduct interviews, and decide whose search services they wish to employ.

Proximity of the selected consultant and board members' and consultant's calendars also affect how long it takes to determine procedural ground rules, gather necessary information about district needs and desired candidate qualifications, and approve brochures and advertisements for dissemination. Frequently, positions are advertised for approximately 2 months prior to the application deadline date. However, several consultants mentioned that if the board does not offer a very high salary, they prefer to extend the number of months that the position is advertised as a means of increasing the number of potential applicants that the vacancy announcement (and informal recruitment) may reach.

Once the application deadline is met, it can take up to 2 months for the consultant to complete his or her paper screening, preliminary interviews, and background checks of applicants. Then, it could take another month to determine, schedule, and complete the first round of in-district interviews of the narrowed field of (typically) five to six candidates. Usually, the second round of in-district interviews occurs within 2 weeks of the first, but again, it varies widely depending on candidates' and board availability, amount of distance to be traveled, and scope of community and other nonboard group involvement in the process.

The same variation holds true for the time between identification of the two or three semifinalists and the final appointment. The board visitation to the tentative finalist's current district of employment also occurs during this period. Throughout each of the various parts of the process, the degree of consensus or dissensus on who should be eliminated from the ever-narrowing slate of candidates significantly affects the amount of time needed for decision making and search completion. Some time will inevitably pass between the date of the final board decision and acceptance of the contract by the successful candidate. And, of course, the time can vary widely between contract signature and the finalist's actual starting date in the new district.

A Subtle Exercise of Influence

Many school board members and consultants describe the superintendent search not only in functional terms (i.e., the means to a hiring decision) but also as a "board development" process. As such, time frames can become more indeterminate, sometimes extending well past the starting date of the newly hired superintendent.

This study's informants mean several different things by board development, in the context of superintendent search and selection. To some, it has to do with board members' professional growth, through becoming better informed about what their internal and external constituencies view as strengths, weaknesses, and desired directions for the schools. To others, it means coming together as a board by reflecting on district needs, short- and long-term goals, and the implications of those needs and goals for district leadership. For some, such reflection is a novel occurrence, because it is commonly necessary to devote much attention to "keeping the district moving," passing budgets, and dealing with the more routine business and governance of board meetings. For others, "coming together" means getting to know one another better than ever before.

Some headhunters are purposeful in structuring such educative opportunities for the boards with whom they consult. Typically, there are two points of intervention seen as key: the initial discussions with the board prior to advertising the vacancy, and the specific training for candidate interviews. Some consultants add a third development service after the newly hired superintendent is on the job.

At the first of these three intervention points, the consultant guides the discussion to bring up both differences and commonalities among board members' perspectives on what is needed and desired for the district. As a part of this conversation, consultants work hard to dig beneath superficial expressions of needs, sometimes employing pointed challenges to board members: "This is what I hear you telling me. Is that really what you want? Might that be a reaction to what you feel was missing in the previous superintendent's skill sets or accomplishments?"

The second point of structured education has been elaborated earlier, in the section on "Preparation for Interviews." Technical and legal compliance information is a big part of this training. However, developing or selecting interview questions can also be an important exercise in clarifying and prioritizing board directions.

The third and less frequently included board development opportunity occurs when some consultants return to the district 1 to 3 months after the new superintendent begins employment. This typically involves a superintendent-school board working session to clarify priorities and performance goals for the first year, and/or to underscore appropriate roles and responsibilities of boards and superintendents. The latter often reinforce norms that "the school board governs and the superintendent administers the district," or, put another way, that the board establishes policy and the superintendent implements that policy and manages the daily operations of the school district (Carter & Cunningham, 1997; Danzberger & Usdan, 1992). Regardless of the specific content of such sessions, the overarching goal is that the superintendent-board relationship start off on solid ground, with clear communication about mutual expectations. As a consultant puts it, "Just sort of making sure that anything that needs to be ironed out gets ironed out in the beginning, and that everybody's moving in the same direction, and there's a common set of expectations about what the board's role is and what the superintendent's role is."

These three recurring types of board education activities during the superintendent search, however, are just the formal, structured pieces of the process. Board development also occurs informally and serendipitously. After all, search and selection involves many months of work, with more frequent meetings and interactions among board members than they are normally accustomed to. As a board member in this study illustrates, "Even at the interview dinners with the three semifinalists, I was learning more about my fellow board members than I ever knew before. It's a more casual setting. And the candidate has to eat! So, that gives the board the opportunity to talk a little bit about ourselves, how we got on the board, why we did this, and what we thought was important to the community and to the schools. We got to know each other very well through that, which I think can be a big plus from the whole experience." This board member was referring to how increased communication and knowledge of others' motivations brought better understanding and cohesiveness to the board.

Some consultants see one of their primary roles as intentionally, though informally, "bringing board members together," either generating or reinforcing a solid working relationship on the board. That is, whereas the board member quote above portrays board cohesiveness as a happy and unanticipated by-product of the search process, in fact, many consultants see themselves as purposefully working to ensure that outcome. A consultant explains, "There's an important *subtle* role—helping the board become more cohesive so that, when the new superintendent comes in, you have a united board. We did that by getting each board member to talk about what they're looking for in a superintendent, and looking for areas of agreement among them. . . . The consultant is a teacher and a facilitator, helping the board understand what they want, and helping them get to know each other and learn to work with each other better."

Of course, sometimes the potential for building cohesion and achieving consensus goes unrealized, regardless of consultants' and individual board members' efforts, whether structured or informal. Some boards start out, and remain, contentious throughout the search process. Some board development never "takes." Some superintendent selections, despite unanimous public votes to the contrary, are made on split decisions.

You, of course, will be enormously curious about all of this. If hired, you may eventually find out what the *real* vote was on your appointment, most likely from a trusted board member. At the time of hiring, you can count on everyone keeping this information from you. You might ask the consultant and board president before you sign the contract, but it's doubtful they will tell you how individual board members voted.

However, you will be able to find out beforehand what the history and general tone of intraboard relationships has been. Usually, contentious or split boards do not develop overnight. Board relationships should routinely be a key part of your homework, prior to submitting an application for any superintendency.

Interim Superintendents' Roles

Typically not thought of as key players in accessing the superintendency, interim superintendents can also exercise considerable influence on your future prospects. Here's what you should know about their formal and informal roles.

Whether related to board dissensus on finalists, difficulties recruiting suitable applicants, or the particular timing of an exiting superintendent's departure, a district's superintendency often needs to be filled temporarily. For this purpose, "interims" may be employed for any time between a month and a year, usually via a per diem or short-term consulting arrangement with the board.

Interims are typically retired superintendents from the local region, although at times, they travel from more distant parts. Sometimes, consultants, other school boards, veteran superintendents, or state board/superintendent associations help identify interims for needy school districts.

Although some boards interview two or more interim candidates, others simply accept their most favored source's recommendation. A school board member puts it succinctly: "Finding the interim? That was easy. We just went to [the regional superintendent], and he used his network of retired superintendents." As a consultant in this study explains, "Finding interims is on the closed side of the process. Sometimes, it's only a phone call to a person I know is available. It's good to know some people and to have a cadre of people that you can depend on to be able to do those kinds of things, usually on fairly short notice."

At the time of hiring an interim, most boards are focused on finding the superintendent's permanent replacement. Consequently, they view the interim as a place-holder—someone who will manage the district's affairs and maintain the status quo. In this study, interim superintendents were found to play a variety of other roles, including both directly and indirectly shaping superintendent search and selection processes.

Let's begin with the most direct influences. As in the second of the vignettes that opened this chapter, interims sometimes gallop to the rescue after the headhunter-assisted search yields no one whom the board finds acceptable. Interims sometimes make contacts of their own and recruit additional candidates for the board to consider and, eventually, hire. They may have very clear, direct influence on the ultimate outcome of the search.

Another illustration of direct intervention is when either the board or the consultant decides that the interim should serve as a second set of eyes, reading through all of the applications and culling the strongest candidates for the board to consider. This, too, is considerable power.

Some interims interview candidates, either as part of group situations with the board or within-district stakeholder committees, or one-on-one (e.g., while shepherding visiting semifinalists on tours of the district). The direct influence emerges when the interim provides feedback to the board on the candidates' relative strengths and weaknesses. Several candidates in this study sensed that they "had it made" with the hiring board when they knew they had favorably impressed the interim. A candidate recounts: "[The interim] took a liking to me, for whatever reason, as part of the interview process. He kept on saying to me that I was going to get the job. I knew he was going to try to influence the board in that respect, but I didn't know how much influence he had. He kept on saying, 'You're what they need and they know it.'"

On the other hand, an interim's disfavor was viewed as an additional hurdle for some candidates to vault on the way to a superintendency. But it is not only candidates' perceptions that suggest interim superintendents' roles in search and selection. Several board members corroborate that it was a trusted interim who helped them determine which finalist would be the better fit for their district. To wit, "It was obvious who the interim's preferred candidate was. To wit, "It was obvious who the interim's preferred candidate was. How happy we would be. How we could not lose if we went with this person. Now, he did not say, 'Oh, you have to pick this one.' And he did not put down the other candidates. But he allayed any concerns or fears we had about his preferred choice. There were a lot of assurances. And we believed him."

And why wouldn't boards believe their interims? They've been superintendents themselves; they're familiar with education laws and customs; they come highly recommended by either another school board or some other trusted professional source; and, in the words of a veteran school board member, "Interims don't have to get to the end of the year and go through a superintendent's evaluation by the board, so they're a little bit freer to speak their minds."

Another board member reflects on the role of the interim superintendent as "a two-edged sword. He did influence the board's thinking. We certainly needed his help. And he brought us ideas and materials he'd tried in the past and elsewhere." Those ideas are sometimes indirect ways of shaping the superintendent search and selection process, including (a) sharing opinions with the board on which consultant to select to run the search and/or how it should be conducted; (b) offering assessments of what the district seems to need; (c) independently investigating candidates' backgrounds and references; (d) generating, or providing lists of, questions to ask of candidates during interviews; (e) serving as a sounding board for individual board members thinking through their evaluations of various applicants; (f) facilitating the board's development (as described earlier) or "decompression," particularly if the previous superintendent left under unpleasant or particularly contentious circumstances; and (g) being a reference point of comparison.

This latter role is distinct from the others, in that here the interim is not the agent of the action but, rather, the object. When he—few females were found to serve as interims in this study—first joins the district, comparisons between his and the recently exited superintendent's style of working invariably surface. Although board members and stakeholders involved in the selection process almost always contrast applicants with their previous superintendent, sometimes, the interim also becomes a standard for comparison.

What you should be aware of is that the comparisons run in both directions. As a board member explains, a bad interim can help any successor look good, even when the expectations are distinctly otherwise: "The feeling in our district was that we would have a 'throw-away' superintendent, because the former superintendent was so re-vered. That did not happen. Maybe it was because our interim was so godawful. He made the next guy coming in look great! That superin-tendent stayed with us 8 years, until his retirement."

In the reverse, if a board grows especially fond of an interim's work style or personality, candidates for successor can suffer by comparison. Of course, any of the interim's influence, direct or indi-rect, is dependent on the board-interim relationship, including the degree of trust, credibility, objectivity, and respect accorded him by the board.

Power and Influence

Much previous research emphasizes the facilitative and educa-tive roles of search consultants with respect to school board decision making about superintendent selection (Afton, 1985; Martin, 1978; Rickabaugh, 1986; Roberts, 1996; Swart, 1990; Tieman, 1968; Wrubel, 1990). Similarly, as I interviewed the 75 informants for this study and made field observations at relevant meetings and conferences, I re-peatedly heard two things. "The consultant does not pick the super-intendent, the school board does" and "It's changed a lot since the times when the real kingmakers had their stables." Let's consider this last statement first.

There are still a number of headhunters who are extraordinarily prolific and/or highly reputed nationally for their search services, connections with top candidates, and prior experience with some of the largest or highest status school districts across the country. As one of them said to me, "Hey, whether you like it or not, when you're a consultant, you exercise a certain amount of power. I mean, that's a given." However, power does appear to be dispersed among more players now than it was in the days when a few elite university-based "placement barons" had a corner on the superintendency market na-tionally and took great pride in their sponsorship of cadres of protégés (Kamler & Shakeshaft, 1998; Magowan, 1979; Tyack & Hansot, 1982). This study confirms what Magowan (1979) predicted more than 20 years ago—that the system of placement barons of the past would be replaced by a "coterie of baronets" (p. 260).

Several factors seem to have contributed to this shift. First, to-day's school boards have grown accustomed to working in a context of shared decision making and constituency involvement in education. A consultant reflects on this change: "I can remember in 1980 a board member calling me up and saying, 'Bring me a superintendent.' That doesn't happen any more. The stakeholders all want to be involved: teachers, staff, community members. Now there are interview teams that see the semifinalists, not just the board. It's a whole different era."

A second and related factor is that as community involvement increases, knowledge of context and leadership skills appropriate for a particular mix of constituencies and issues becomes salient. Another veteran consultant explains, "The old 'stables' were based on the assumption that because you were blessed by one of the powerbrokers, you were going to have access to every district, everywhere. You could count on being taken to any board. But the assumptions we're operating on now are that every district is different. And the strengths a candidate has might be appropriate for one district but not another." This perspective parallels a shift in theory that has characterized the preparation of school administrators, from a "trait" approach, which emphasized personal charisma or other individual attributes, to an emphasis on "situational" leadership skills and the uniqueness of school and district cultures (Bredeson, 1996; Hoyle, 1993; Starratt, 1996). Johnson's (1996) studies of new superintendents underscore the value of this link between leadership and context.

A third factor that may have contributed to the shift from a few placement barons with their cadres of preferred candidates to a more diffuse network of power and influence relates to quantity—numbers of applicants and numbers of semifinalists that school boards expect to meet. In the words of one consultant, "We don't have the problem of stables anymore. We're all too busy looking for horses!" O'Connell's (1995) research indicates widespread concern among search consultants in New York for what they see as dwindling pools of applicants. McAdams (1998) cites a growing body of anecdotal evidence that superintendency candidates are becoming harder to find nationwide. Yet school boards still expect to see five or six strong candidates for each search. As a headhunter observes, "The days of going out and headhunting for a candidate or two to bring to a board are over. They'd fire you in a minute if you tried that."

A fourth factor may be related to trends in the composition of the educational administration professoriate. Although in recent decades, there have never been high percentages of professors with previous experience as superintendents, the proportion seems to be decreasing rather than remaining stable or increasing. McCarthy and Kuh's (1997, p. 87) research on educational administration professors throughout North America indicates that in 1986, 24% of their respondents had served previously as superintendents; by 1994, that proportion had dropped to 17%. Interestingly, even though colleges and universities do not have as many former superintendents on their faculty as in the past, they are employing more faculty who have been school administrators of other kinds: Thirty-seven percent of the 1994 faculty respondents had previously served as "other K-12 administrators," up from 28% in 1986 (McCarthy & Kuh, 1997, p. 87). Together, these figures may be compared to 30 years ago, when "in the mid-1960s, 90% of educational administration faculty members were drawn from the ranks of practitioners" (McCarthy & Kuh, 1997, p. 256).

Nevertheless, the fact that elite university-based placement barons with stables of candidates are less evident now than they were in the past does not mean that a system of powerbrokers that influences access to the superintendency no longer exists (Kamler & Shakeshaft, 1998; Moody, 1983). Tyack and Hansot's (1982) observations about practices in the 1920s and 1930s remain equally true today: "The sponsor was a powerbroker only if the school board recognized his authority" (p. 141). The research reported in this volume demonstrates that school boards continue to depend on search consultants and afford them ample power and authority, particularly in the screening and winnowing parts of the selection process. This brings us to the other recurrent theme emphasized in the practitioner literature (e.g., Chion-Kenney, 1994; Johnson, 1975; Krinsky, 1992) and corroborated by board member and headhunter informants in this study: that the consultant does not pick the superintendent, the school board does.

Yes, the school board does decide whom it will hire as superintendent. However, it makes that choice primarily by interviewing a small number of candidates, after relying on its search consultant to eliminate almost 90% of those who apply. This percentage is derived from comparing the average number of applicants per search (40, as reported in the research of O'Connell, 1995) to the number of semifinalists typically interviewed by school boards (five or six). Hence, this is considerable power for individual headhunters and calls into question the oversimplicity of the axiom that it is the school board that "picks" the superintendent.

But as this and other studies show (e.g., Miklos, 1988; Rose, 1969), consultants do not work alone. This chapter and previous chapters have detailed how and when consultants use their networks of trusted associates to help find, evaluate, promote, and eliminate applicants (Kamler, 1995; Magowan, 1979; Radich, 1992; Wheatley, 1979). I use the plural intentionally (networks) because this system of interconnections has multiple layers. The smallest and most directly influential is the layer composed of the consultants themselves.

The second and largest layer is the extended web of informants relied upon for reference checks and recruitment of candidates. It includes local and regional superintendents (whether incumbent or retired), administrators, and professors of educational administration. In his study, Swart (1990) refers to this element of the process as "network screening," as distinguishable from "paper screening."

A third layer is composed of the ex-superintendent interims who work with boards closely, although temporarily, during the period of time that the board is immersed in the process of selecting a new superintendent. This third element is one never before reported in prior research, and it may be a unique contribution of this study warranting future investigation.

As a consultant reports, "Sure, we talk with each other all the time. We check with each other all the time. We'd be foolish not to." Why foolish? Because although usually not sustaining an identifiable stable of candidates, all consultants need to develop and maintain their knowledge of "who's out there, who might be interested, and what their abilities are." And it is the participants in this multilayered network who provide that information.

Headhunters, savvy school board members, candidates, and school administrators understand how influential these networks are to accessing the superintendency. A candidate who was successful in obtaining a superintendency recalls, "I knew that just sending in applications and hoping would not get me where I wanted to go, and that politics and connections are involved in getting these positions." Another explains matter-of-factly, "There's a very powerful network of superintendents and consultants that strongly influence the movement of superintendents in our state. I try to make my work known to as many of them as I can." It's "how the system works."

There are features specific to common search and selection practices that contribute to the enduring strengths of this system. As described earlier, these include norms of informal recruitment for candidate pools, boards' reliance on consultants to screen applications and narrow the field for them, interpretive leeway in screening allowed by both the unwritten criteria that come into play and the breadth of stated qualifications hoped for in candidates, consultants' use of multiple sources for background checking of applicants, and traditions of mentoring and sponsorship of novice administrators by veterans and superordinates.

There are also structural factors that contribute to keeping the system intact (Wheatley, 1981). For example, many states are divided into county or regional supervisory/service areas, sometimes called "intermediate units" (Campbell, Cunningham, Nystrand, & Usdan, 1990). The administrators who head those units are usually in close contact with their area school boards, administrators, and schools; some meet regularly on a statewide basis to share information and problem solve together. As a consultant explains, "These can be among the tightest networks in some states. They are in contact with each other frequently and pretty much know everybody who's out there." A regional superintendent reports, "Our networking system is remarkable. We're right up front with each other about Candidate X, Y, or Z because we know them. And we can paint a very accurate picture of all the districts in the state."

Other structures that support these networks are the state and national professional organizations of superintendents and administrators. These associations are designed to help their members connect, support, and share information with one another. Employment and career development are but two of countless other issues with which these organizations are concerned. Nevertheless, the formal and informal communications that such organizations foster are key institutionalized structures for the exchange of information about superintendent candidates.

Summary and Implications

This chapter had two principal foci. The first centered on what potential future candidates for the superintendency should know about how final stages of the selection process often unfold. Discussion included practical advice about understanding and handling gaps in communication, lags in time, contract negotiations, appointment announcements, and board dissensus about the hiring decision.

The second focus was on how overt and subtle forces of power come into play in these processes. Illustrations of various forms of influence and powerbrokering were discussed, both as current phenomena and within historical context. It was pointed out that, although the informal systems of connections that influence access to the superintendency are sometimes fluid and amorphous, there also exist institutionalized structures that support and sustain them.

One of the dilemmas that you and other potential superintendents will inevitably face in your career is whether to dissociate from, resist, or use (and, therefore, reinforce) these informal networks of power and influence. Obviously, the advice given in this volume so far has assumed that you will be employing, rather than resisting or dissociating yourself from, these systems.

But you should also understand the moral dimension to this dilemma, for which simplistic tips and unambiguous counsel do not apply. That is, when professional networks work to the advantage of all talented, able candidates, they are likely to flourish unquestioned and may appear to be natural, perhaps even efficient, ways of functioning. When such systems advance the prospects of questionably competent individuals or ignore the talents of others, they can be viewed as exclusive and unfair.

It's important to appreciate both of these potentials for the webs of connections that influence access to the superintendency. For this reason, the second half of this volume is dedicated to a more critical analysis of common search and selection practices. The conceptual emphases in Part 2 are gender equity and racial/ethnic diversity.

Part II

Preventing and Promoting Advancement

4

What Do Sex and Color
Have to Do With It?

Eric Rower, search consultant, is making a presentation at the annual conference of the National Association of School Administrators. The session is titled "Aspiring Superintendents: How to Get
the Job You Want." Administrators from all parts of the country are in
attendance. Eric explains that he's been assisting school boards with
superintendent searches for 26 years, is committed to increasing the
representation of women and minorities in the superintendency, and
has worked with boards from 31 of the 50 states. He describes the experiential background of what he judges to be the best candidates:

> My model is Dr. Bob Nichols in the Truman school district. He
> was a teacher 3 to 5 years. He became a principal, a secondary
> principal, for 3 to 4 years. At age 31, he had his doctorate out of
> [private] university. Then, he got himself a superintendency in a
> small district. He stayed there 4 to 5 years. Then, he went to a
> larger district for his second superintendency. Then to his cur-
> rent [affluent, suburban] district. He's been a superintendent
> now for a total of about 25 years! He went through the chairs, but
> he never stayed 10-15 years in any of them. Not that you *have* to
> go through the chairs. That's not necessary. But that's the *quickest*
> way. Now look at the other patterns [in candidates' experiential
> background] you see today! Many of them teach too long. When
> you teach 10, 15, 20 years, you get socialized into the norms of
> teaching. Now, in my book, administrators *are* teachers. But
> teach 5 to 8 years, then move on. Then, get an assistant principal-
> ship for 2 or 3 years. If you stay 3 years, you've been there too
> long, unless you want to make that your career. But if you want to

move up, get the hell out of an assistant principalship. Take a principalship for 5 or 6 years, then move into the central office. Again, that's the *quickest* way to go [to the superintendency] but it's not the *only* way to go. . . . Now, if you've taught for 15 years and haven't even gotten into a principalship yet, or some other central office position, when you finally get to that superintendency position, you're 50 years old. So now you're in the twilight of your career. Now boards don't, and it's illegal to, discriminate by age. But I would say, my observation over the years, is that there's an advantage to being young.

What does this description communicate to aspiring superintendents? How do gender and race relate to these preferred career trajectories? What else do we know about how "quality" is defined by the key decision makers in superintendent selection: school board members and headhunters? What are the implications for you, a potential future candidate for the superintendency?

This chapter will answer these questions by drawing upon both my own and others' research. It will also examine the broader sociopolitical contexts relevant to accessing this important educational leadership role.

Understanding Career Pathways

First, you should know that Eric's perspective on the ideal career path was common in this study and has a long history in the educational administration profession. Experiential background dominates initial decision making about the "best" candidates to move forward in search and selection processes (Schmuck & Wyant, 1981). This background is often defined in terms of prior service in particular administrative roles, most frequently principalships, central office positions, and other superintendencies—in that order. In the field vernacular, this job movement is referred to as "moving up" or "moving through" the "chairs" (Black & English, 1986, 1996; Carter, Glass, & Hord, 1993).

You also need to be aware that the assessment of the quality of that prior experience is often shaped by more specific concerns about the contexts in which the experiences are acquired. The contextual variables that appear to be key are size (of school, district, or administrative unit) and type of community (rural, suburban, or urban). With respect to the former, ever-increasing size is equated with appropriate career progress. Regarding type of community, it is assumed that leadership demands in rural, suburban, and urban districts are sufficiently distinct to warrant weighing more heavily experience in the same type of district as the one doing the hiring. That is, if an urban district is hiring a new superintendent, that board and consultant will be more likely to favor candidates with prior experience in urban, rather than suburban or rural, districts.

In this study, headhunters, candidates, and school board members explained that these contextual "matches" are important to the boards and stakeholder screening committees involved in superintendent selection. As illustrated in Eric Rower's remarks, they are also important to some consultants. This point is echoed in the advice that another headhunter frequently gives to prospective superintendent candidates: "It's tough to jump across lines. If you want to change type of district, maybe you shouldn't look at a superintendency first. Get experience early on in your career, and go through the chairs there, in the same type of district you want to be a superintendent in [urban-suburban-rural]."

At times, these preferences for progressions through particular administrative roles, in settings of particular sizes and community types, are accompanied by a concomitant devaluing of lengthy experience in classroom teaching or in any one of the administrative roles viewed as appropriate stepping stones to the superintendency. Also, in some cases, administrative experience at the secondary level is valued more highly than equivalent experience at the elementary level. (More on this later in the chapter.)

This perspective on preferred experience has enjoyed regular reinforcement in journal articles and texts aimed at advising novice administrators about fruitful pathways to obtaining a superintendency (Black & English, 1986, 1996; Carter et al., 1993; Natale, 1992). For example, Glass (1993) describes the "natural" superintendent career path as

a sequence of positions and experiences [that] tends to occur in a logical and ordered progression of positions of increasing responsibility and complexity. A small portion of superintendents, especially women, have been observed to deviate from this somewhat "natural" progression. But . . . some variation in career from the norm is not unexpected. (p. 30)

Let's look deeper. As you will recall, it is the headhunters who often make the first cut of superintendent candidates, eliminating anywhere between 5 and 100 applications before forwarding (typically) 10 to 12 on which the school board can focus. What happens when the best qualified are pictured in this way by some of the highest producing search consultants? How might we analyze more critically these depictions of natural and model experiential backgrounds, one from recent literature and one illustrative of many consultant informants in this study? What do these perspectives say about candidates who deviate from the preferred pathways?

First, such candidates are something other than "ideal" or "model." Instead, they are "slow" or, at the least, "slower" than those on the "quickest" track to the superintendency. Some may be overly immersed in the "norms of teaching," which, by implication, are somehow inferior to or less desirable than the norms of administration. Clearly, the preferred sequence of job changes is from building-level to district-level administrative positions, thereby making other patterns less highly regarded. And finally, there appear to be distinct disadvantages to being middle-aged, rather than younger, when seeking one's first superintendency, even though school boards and consultants do not practice age discrimination. Age 50 is viewed as the twilight of the ideal career path, not the time to start looking for a school superintendency.

Age and prior experience. This perspective on age is particularly disadvantageous to females. Some background information helps explain why.

Glass's (1992) research indicates that "women generally are appointed to their first administrative positions later than men" (p. 58). Shakeshaft (1989) reports that women in educational administration "tend to be in their mid- to late 40s. . . . The higher the position they hold, the older they are" (p. 57). Glass (1992) also finds that the majority of male superintendents (59.9%) begin their administrative careers between the ages of 25 and 30; the majority of female superintendents (53.9%) enter administration between ages 31 and 40 (p. 59).

In previous research I conducted with a colleague, we found that women entered their first superintendencies in New York State an average of four years later than men: females at age 46, males at age 42 (O'Connell & Tallerico, 1998). Relatedly, Glass (1992) found that "women superintendents, on average, spend a longer time as classroom teachers than do men. . . . Twice as many female as male superintendents have spent 10 or more years in the classroom" (p. 58). Shakeshaft (1989) cites research indicating that "the average woman principal spends fifteen years as a teacher before seeking a principalship, whereas the average male spends five" (p. 63).

Although no national statistics are available on the age distributions of men and women in university-based administrator preparation programs, anecdotal evidence from U.S. professors of educational administration indicates a sharp shift in student demographics during the past 20 to 25 years—from predominantly males, in their late 20s or early 30s, to predominantly females, in their late 30s and early 40s. Current demographics, and their relationship to superintendent career paths, are brought to life by one of the professor-headhunters in this study:

> I don't know what you find in your Educational Administration program, but our typical person entering now is a 40- to 42-year-old female who has been teaching 17 years and doesn't want to be a principal. With that pool entering their studies today, and the traditional notion that you've got to go through the chairs, what are we looking at? We're looking at 54- and 55-year-old women looking for their first superintendencies. Boards say, "Why hire them? In another year, they'll be eligible to retire, and we'll be out looking again." So is there age discrimination? Yes. Absolutely. For men and for women. But it's particularly more acute for women because many of them start their administrative career path later. . . . Does that limit women for getting into the superintendency? Absolutely. . . . Of course, the variable there is child bearing and child rearing.

Besides further illustrating the relationships between professional licensure, age, and career experience, this excerpt reveals the consultant's awareness of differential impacts and explanations by gender. For example, if women are older than men when they apply for their first superintendency, then overt or subtle age discrimination will affect them more significantly. Moreover, women administrators' lengthier teaching experience than men's may be explained by the fact that the typical workday of teachers is compatible with children's school-day schedules and, therefore, may be conducive to a combination of career and child rearing (Shakeshaft, 1989). It is clear that additional studies examining the interrelationship of age, gender, race/ethnicity, and experience could help shed more light on the issue of accessing advanced-level leadership positions such as the superintendency.

Some previous research suggests that, as middle-aged males are thinking of winding down their careers and finding fulfillment outside of work, women who have raised children often seek new career challenges and adult connections through work outside the home when their children reach their teens and they themselves are in their 40s and 50s (Krupp, 1983, 1991; Levine, 1989). Thus, a particular age that may appear to be the twilight of an educational career for males may not be that at all for female administrators and superintendent candidates. Is it fair to judge the latter through an age-career path lens that has come to be seen as the "quickest" and the "best," based mostly on the fact that that's the path many male superintendents have traveled in the past?

High school principal experience. Another experiential factor that may also be a residual of the typical career path of past male superintendents is the secondary principalship. A search consultant captures the point well when he says, "The high school principalship has been a traditional training ground for superintendents." More than half of all headhunters and school board members who participated in this study reported that prior experience as a high school principal was valued more highly than was elementary principalship experience in superintendent selection. As one consultant put it bluntly, "Whether it's right or wrong is moot. It's a reality!"

It's also a good example of how unwritten rules affect search and selection processes. That is, it is rare to see the secondary principalship listed in superintendent vacancy announcements as a preferred or required qualification. Instead, it is common to see advertised expectations for both "building-level and central office administrative experience." Specificity about the grade level of that building-level experience occurs primarily in the private conversations that boards, consultants, and selection committees share.

There are a number of reasons why high school principals are favored. In comparison to the elementary principalship, the high school role is viewed as more complex and is characterized by more visible pressures and more difficult problems. These problems include students' drinking, smoking, chemical abuse, dropping out, sexual activity, pregnancy, and a whole variety of misbehaviors and rebelliousness that sometimes inspire severe disciplinary actions, such as suspensions and expulsions from school. These are exactly the kinds of issues that attract local media attention.

Also, high school athletics, interscholastic competitions of other sorts, and celebratory events such as proms and commencement ceremonies are high-visibility activities that often elicit much community interest. Secondary schools also tend to attract greater attention than do elementary schools because accountability for academic performance involves several high stakes: graduation or not, acceptance to or rejection by colleges, employment or unemployment after graduation. The power of much of this high-stakes decision making is frequently associated with the secondary school principal.

But student issues are not the only factors in this mix. Teacher union leadership and activism are often centered at this level. And teachers themselves are perceived as more troublesome to manage at that level, given their greater allegiances to particular departments and content specialties rather than to the school organization as a whole (Corwin & Borman, 1988). Taken together, all of these difficulties and complexities contribute to the perception that a secondary principalship may provide better preparation for the pressure-packed, political world of the superintendent than any other building-level experiences. A vivid expression of this point of view comes from a consultant who routinely conducts two or three superintendent searches per year, and has been doing so for 14 years.

> There's a big difference between serving as a high school principal and serving as an elementary principal. . . . It's almost like you've been to Vietnam and back again if you've been a high school principal. And you were only exposed to the Korean War in the elementary principalship. That's the board bias. And guess what? I tend to agree.

The military metaphor embedded here may be telling. Are men and women equally likely to fit into this person's warrior imagery? It's doubtful. Who tends to benefit from these models of the ideal experiential background? Probably white males, because their careers are more likely to follow the path described as normative by many of the informants for this study (Glass, 1992; Grogan & Henry, 1995; Ortiz, 1982; Shakeshaft, 1989).

We know, for example, that higher percentages of female and minority principals are found at the elementary rather than the secondary levels (Montenegro, 1993). We also know that, nationally, the highest proportions of female administrators are in coordinator and director roles—positions more typically associated with centralized, rather than building-based, administrative functions (Hodgkinson & Montenegro, 1999; Montenegro, 1993; Ortiz, 1982; Tallerico, 1997). Moreover, such positions are more likely to be entered directly from teaching, without a principalship required. We know that women are likely to have spent more years in teaching than men, prior to moving into their first administrative job (Shakeshaft, 1989). Relatedly, this makes women, as a group, older than male candidates for the various chairs leading to the superintendency. Again, this is an area ripe for additional research in the future.

Prior superintendencies. Of course, when previous experience as a superintendent is required, that significantly increases the chances that a white male, rather than a female or nonmajority male, will meet the preferred experiential background criteria. Additionally, we know that, historically, higher proportions of female superintendents than male superintendents have occupied superintendencies in the smallest local school districts across the United States (Ortiz & Marshall, 1988; Tallerico & Burstyn, 1996), thereby giving the size-progression advantage to males. In an illustration by a suburban school board member: "There were three female candidates among the 50 or so who applied. And of the three, none of them met the criteria for experience we wanted. Again, we were of the mindset that 'We're a wonderful district, we've had a wonderful superintendent. We want God to come here.' We were looking for a very strong resumé, a lot of experience, including a superintendency. Now I don't know if those females exist, or they didn't apply, or they didn't hear about our vacancy. But none that we got met our criteria."

Career Paths and Selection Practices

It is more than just the mind-sets that screeners bring to superintendent selection that matter. There are a number of specific practices within the search process that reinforce these idealized pictures and career pathways. One important practice is recruitment. As detailed in previous chapters, most consultants do not simply sit back, wait for candidates to apply, and then screen out those who exhibit "deficiencies" in prior experience. Rather, they actively recruit prospective applicants to ensure that the board for which they are working has a solid pool of qualified semifinalists from which to make its selection. Recruitment offers fertile territory for the enactment of one's predispositions about "best qualified." As a consultant explains, "We don't go in thinking we'll only bring the board a certain kind of candidate. But once experienced superintendents don't emerge in the pool, then we go looking and recruiting. And that's where these preferences for past experiences come in."

Beyond recruitment, there are several more mechanical parts of search and selection practices that reinforce a "best" and historically male administrative career pathway to the superintendency. For example, many consultants' surveys of community and employee groups include detailed inquiries about previous positions that respondents would like to see in the backgrounds of superintendent candidates whom they would consider top contenders. Other survey items inquire about the size and type of school (elementary, secondary) or district (rural, suburban, urban) in which the ideal candidate should have experience. Similarly, consultants often sort applicants into discrete categories, organizing candidate files into separate piles for consideration by the school board or selection committee: one pile for those with prior superintendent experience, one for those with building-level experience, and one for those with both building-level and district office experience. Both of these practices reify the centrality of particular previous positions (e.g., principal, assistant superintendent, superintendent) and deflect attention from leadership skills that may be acquired in a wide variety of administrative roles (e.g., interpersonal communications, knowledge of curriculum and human resource development, conflict management capabilities).

Also, many consultants summarize data about applicants in spreadsheets whose major categories focus on prior administrative positions, name and size of district, and number of years in each position, thus further underscoring the salience of particular job sequences and size progressions. For applicants screened out early in the process by the consultant, these summary spreadsheets are often the only source of information attended to by the school board. That is, most school board members do not scrutinize the original files of applicants already judged inadequately qualified by their search consultant. (After all, they are paying the consultants to accomplish this labor-intensive piece of the process.) Instead, boards rely on the consultant's abbreviated summaries, which again often characterize candidates in terms of previous positions held, rather than in terms of the leadership skills sought/advertised as selection qualifiers. In this way, unwritten selection criteria and taken-for-granted assumptions about appropriate career paths become powerful factors in determining which candidates advance to the all-important board interview stage of the search and selection process.

These factors also relate to who gets recruited for which superintendency vacancies. In the example that follows, a consultant summarizes both the district-size and administrative-position progressions that lead to the most desirable superintendencies. Deviations from these normative progressions may not preclude the candidate from a superintendency, but they can limit opportunities to districts lowest in the hierarchy of relative status. "I mean, you start out in a small district, and then you move to the bigger, more metropolitan districts. And if your background doesn't look like the typical principal-central office-superintendent, then you're even more likely to get the smallest or most remote superintendency for your first one."

A Broader Conceptual Framework

So far, this chapter has focused on the predominance of a specific sequence of administrative experiences in how quality is often defined in superintendent selection. What's important to understand is that many forces influencing access to the superintendency are extrinsic to you as an individual applicant. Riehl and Byrd's (1997) research suggests multiple levels of social and political influences that shape differential access to educational administrative jobs for males and females. One way to think about these interrelated dynamics is to visualize a nested series of concentric circles (see Figure 4.1).

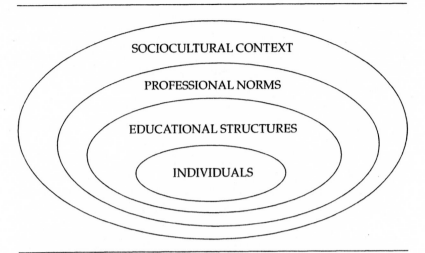

Figure 4.1. The Interrelationship of Social and Political Influences on Administrative Job Access

At the center, the smallest circle is individual agency. This includes elements such as your personal and professional experiences, aspirations, ambitions, abilities, values, family responsibilities, and geographic mobility.

The next wider concentric circle emphasizes educational structures. Some of these were mentioned in Chapter 3, such as systems of administrative recruitment common to the field of education; institutionalized regularities in superintendent selection; and statewide organizational units of governance and professional organizations of administrators, both of which serve as information networks. Riehl and Byrd (1997) would likely also include in this layer the structure of opportunities in the field of education, and the presence or absence of role models in educational organizations who look like the prospective applicant. Schmuck's (1981) and Yeakey, Johnston, and Adkison's (1986) research confirms the importance of organizational influences for educational leaders, as does Bell's (1988) for superintendents, in particular.

The next wider concentric circle focuses on the professional norms of educational administration. It includes traditions of mentoring and sponsorship for advancement into and up through the profession (Grogan, 1996; Rose, 1969; Tyack & Hansot, 1982); how novices are socialized into educational administration (Ortiz, 1982; Ortiz &

Marshall, 1988); norms of tokenism, wherein the relatively small numbers of nontraditional candidates in any leadership role tend to both lack informal support systems and be faced with extraordinary scrutiny and performance pressures, creating barriers to the minority person's full integration into historically male fields (Kanter, 1977); and expectations of paying one's dues and advancing through particular chairs toward the superintendency (Black & English, 1986, 1996).

The widest circle in Figure 4.1 encompasses the cultural context of American society. Riehl and Byrd (1997) include within cultural influences the political, ethical, and social climate; occupational and sex role stereotypes endemic to society; and labor market conditions.

Application. How can this conceptual framework be applied in ways relevant to accessing the superintendency? Taken together, these various interacting levels of influence help explain the enduring sameness in the demographic profile of school superintendents during the past 100 years (Crowson, 1987; Tyack & Hansot, 1982). (Specific statistics will be provided later.) That is, there are powerful (although largely invisible) influences within the educational system, the administrative profession, and society that reflect and reinforce long-standing traditions of Caucasian male leadership of American institutions (Banks, 1995; Yeakey et al., 1986).

This model also suggests that access to the superintendency is shaped by forces both intrinsic and extrinsic to the individual. For example, Edson's (1988) research shows that individuals' administrative career aspirations are not formed in a vacuum, independent of historic and present-day opportunity structures and cultural traditions about who occupies educational leadership roles. Rather, they are shaped by personal choices and factors such as cultural norms regarding women's and men's roles in the home, differential expectations (by sex) for child rearing and elder care, and differences in how girls and boys are socialized in our society.

More on professional and sociocultural norms. Tyack and Hansot's (1982) historical research adds to this mix of professional and cultural norms the influence of the ideology of meritocracy. What does this mean? Ideologies may be thought of as widespread belief systems characteristic of a particular society. Meritocracy is defined as "government, leadership or control by people of the highest ability, selected by some form of competition" (Ehrlich, Flexner, Carruth, & Hawkins, 1980, p. 416). The concept of meritocracy is linked with several values embedded in American culture: that hard work and initiative lead to success; that individuals are masters of their own destiny; that possibilities are limitless; and that the most honorable way to advance is to lift oneself up by one's own bootstraps. With respect, more specifically, to employment opportunities, the ideology of meritocracy is also interrelated with the following values: that anyone can get ahead, given enough effort and the appropriate aspirations; that competition operates like Darwinian natural selection, with the most able surviving and the strongest progressing; that individual competence is the key determinant of career advancement; and that the proverbial cream rises naturally to the top.

Most of these values are grounded more in conventional wisdom, myth, and majority cultural assumptions than in current realities (Greene, 1998; Shakeshaft, 1998; Tyack & Hansot, 1982). A significant reality that these assumptions ignore is that connections and sponsorship (not individual competence alone) do matter in obtaining employment and advancement. This is true not only in educational administration but in many other fields of professional employment. Previous research (Grogan, 1996; Hudson, 1994; Rose, 1969), along with the examples shared in the first part of this book, provide ample evidence of the salience of networks of informants and sponsors for accessing the superintendency.

Acting affirmatively. Another element of the American sociocultural context is that these are unfriendly times for affirmative action. This unfriendliness was reflected in many ways in this study.

For example, a retired superintendent who typically conducts two or three superintendent searches per year recounts how a previous State Commissioner of Education encouraged consultants to actively seek diversity in the field of candidates that they provide for school boards. "I raised my hand when he said that at that meeting and said, 'I'll be darned if you're going to tell me who will be a finalist. I won't just put minorities into the finalist pool. I'm always going to go with the best qualified.'"

This perspective suggests that the active pursuit of diversity implies both an unfair advantage for minority candidates and diminished qualifications. However, as detailed previously, many search consultants routinely engage in active recruitment strategies to

ensure a solid pool of semifinalists to forward to school boards or selection committees to interview. For some, the contradiction seems to
go unnoticed that it's OK to target and aggressively pursue the
highly reputed sitting superintendent in another school district (who
is most likely to be a white male), but the notion of purposefully aim-
ing to attract women and minority candidates (that is, acting affirmatively) is somehow suspect, unfair, or likely to be associated with inferior candidate qualifications.

Additionally, acting affirmatively seems to be defined in practice
as granting special favor to women and people of color, rather than
as intentional pursuit and encouragement of qualified, nontraditional candidates. The following consultant's example illustrates
how "merit" and "diversity" are sometimes implied to be opposites:
"Sometimes, boards will ask me, 'How do you feel about female candidates?' This may sound harsh to you, but what I tell them is I'm going to bring the best candidates forward for this job. If it's six women,
fine. But it won't be because there just aren't going to be six women
applying. If it's six men, then it's six men. I will not bring somebody
up because they are female or because they are black or because
they're Hispanic."

It may be that many of this study's informants are both reflecting
and reinforcing a predominant societal viewpoint, because the national climate is currently not supportive of affirmative action in
employment, resource allocation, or college admissions. In K-12 education generally, concerns for equity have been largely displaced by
an almost exclusive focus on excellence (Clark & Astuto, 1986; Jackson, 1995).

Moreover, there is evidence of a national backlash regarding affirmative action policies and practice. For example, in 1996, voters in
California passed Proposition 209, a ballot initiative that essentially
bans any preferences based on race or sex in state hiring, contracting,
or admission to public colleges and universities. The following year,
the U.S. Supreme Court refused to hear the case brought to it by those
opposed to the Proposition. Bell and Chase (1993) also point out that,
since President Reagan's era, monitoring and enforcement of equity
and equal opportunity employment policies have been fragmented
and intermittent at best.

You've come a long way, baby. In part, the current disfavor of affirmative action and other special efforts to remedy historical inequities

associated with race, ethnicity, and gender may be related to improvements in the personal, social, and economic well-being of blacks, women, and other traditionally disadvantaged groups in the past several decades (Dovidio, Kawakami, & Johnson, 1997).

Several studies reveal that women have increased their numbers in the superintendency in the past 25 years. For example, Blount (1998) found that, whereas just 0.70% of all U.S. local superintendents were female in 1970, women's representation in the superintendency increased to 3.94% in 1990. Similarly, Hodgkinson and Montenegro's (1999) research finds 1.0% of all superintendencies occupied by women in 1980; 4.0% in 1988; 7.1% in 1993; and 12% in 1998.

This study's informants frequently lauded these gains and assumed continued increases in the future. For example, a school board member predicts: "I think probably in the next 10 years we will see a lot more women as superintendents, because there are a lot more women in middle management right now. I would just see that the logical next steps for them would be a superintendency. And I think there are four or five in the state now." (Actually, there were 105 female superintendents in her state at the time she shared this thought.)

Many consultants and candidates echo this board member's optimism about women administrators' progress over time. As a female consultant explains, "More women are moving up. I'm seeing more women in high school principalships. I'm certainly seeing a lot more women in the central office than ever before. So, I think that women are gradually moving themselves into those positions of leadership. And I think they also are knowingly doing this. Understanding that that's what they have to do in order to get the top job, if that's their goal."

Similarly, a female candidate currently in her second superintendency relates: "It's very encouraging. I've been in the business 20 years, and I've seen massive changes. A real breaking down of barriers and a real acceptance of females as capable administrators."

Information about race/ethnicity and the superintendency also illustrates small, incremental gains in recent decades. Hodgkinson and Montenegro (1999) report that racial minorities made up about 2.2% of all U.S. superintendents in 1981-1982, increasing to about 3.5% in 1992-1993 and about 5.0% in 1998. (The 1998 figure includes 2.0% African American, 2.0% Hispanic, 1.0% American Indian, and less than half of 1% Asian or Pacific Islander.)

Unfortunately, no long-term trend information on the superintendency, disaggregated by both sex and race/ethnicity, is available. Some researchers refer to this absence as an intentional "conspiracy of silence" (Shakeshaft, 1998; Tyack & Hansot, 1982). Another aspect of this silence is that the published educational administration research that does include people of color tends to focus predominantly on African Americans. (This is a limitation of this book's case study data as well.) With the notable exception of Flora Ida Ortiz's work on Hispanic female superintendents (Ortiz, 1991, 1998), we know little about other people of color in this important role.

Bell and Chase's (1993) research was the first to provide disaggregated data to make a short-term comparison by both race/ethnicity and sex. Contrasting 1989-1990 and 1991-1992, they found increases in the numbers of female Black, Hispanic, Asian, and American Indian superintendents of K-12 districts in the United States. These national data support this study's informants' perceptions of increased representation of women and people of color in the superintendency in the past two to three decades.

Taken together, this optimism about recent gains made by nontraditional candidates and distaste for affirmative action combine to reinforce the meritocracy ideology that the best qualified individuals rise naturally to the top. These beliefs relate directly to the concepts that formed the first half of this chapter: how "best qualified" is defined with respect to viable candidacy for the school superintendency. What else do we know about how quality and merit are understood?

Race and gender neutrality. An earlier discussion noted that multiple layers of forces both shape and constrain the prospects for individual administrative aspirants (see Figure 4.1). However, Chase and Bell (1990, 1994) found that school board members and search consultants sometimes focus exclusively on individuals' skills, effort, and achievements. Such emphases deflect attention away from broader social, cultural, and professional influences; instead, any needed changes are an individual, rather than collective, responsibility (Yeakey et al., 1986). Chase and Bell (1994) also point out that these taken-for-granted foci subtly "conceal the systemic barriers" that women and people of color face "in their attempts to achieve positions of power" (p. 40). Thus, school boards' and consultants' beliefs contribute to sustaining the status quo in the demographics of the school superintendency (Chase & Bell, 1990).

In this study, I routinely inquired about the demographic diversity of the slate of superintendent candidates forwarded to the school board by the consultant, as well as the board's ultimate hiring decision. The gist of the most frequent response to these queries, from both headhunters and school board members alike, was that "we were simply looking for the best qualified people, regardless of their sex or the color of their skin." Such responses echo Chase and Bell's (1990, 1994) findings, reiterate the ideology of individual merit, and add the notions of gender and race neutrality (Ortiz & Marshall, 1995).

The latter assume that sex and race/ethnicity are irrelevant in social interaction, are nonproblematic features of American life, and have little to do with who typically get to be leaders. However, the enduring numerical predominance of Caucasian males in educational leadership and other professions suggests otherwise (Linn, 1998; Wheatley, 1981). For example, according to the U.S. Department of Labor, Caucasian males hold almost 90% of positions in management. In fact, sex and race continue to matter in our culture (Bailey, 1998; Greene, 1998). It is not yet a level playing field.

Relatedly, other scholars point out that assertions of gender and color blindness are sexist and racist in themselves (Rush, 1998; Scheurich & Young, 1998). The rationale is that such assertions are fictions that again serve to shift attention away from problematic social and organizational features, and also perpetuate the status quo—which is inequitable in many economic, social, educational, and political aspects of American life.

Summary and Implications

What do sex and color have to do with accessing the superintendency? According to the research and theoretical framework presented in this chapter, plenty. Relevant issues range from tacit understandings of how "best qualified" is defined by key decision makers in superintendent selection; to how these definitions can be a disadvantage for female and minority administrators; to predominant American belief systems associated with merit, race, and gender.

Intentionally, this chapter has offered few suggestions about what you, as a potential future applicant, might do about all this (at least, at the time of candidacy). The advice that can be inferred from the chapter's opening vignette is, "Increase your chances by ensuring that your career trajectory mirrors a highly valued pathway: teacher, high school principal, and central office administrator."

However, a major construct of the theoretical framework detailed here (Figure 4.1) was that there are such complex dynamics at work that you, as an individual, will never be able to harness all of the forces that come into play in accessing the superintendency. Implications for individual action are limited because there are critical influences largely extrinsic to your locus of control. This is the principal lesson of this chapter.

Overall, the chapter provided a broad conceptual grounding for the more specific, subsequent illustrations of practices that help and hinder equity in access to the superintendency. These are the issues to which we turn our attention next. Chapter 5 will focus on the hindrances, and Chapter 6 on the supports.

5

Where Are the Biases?

Marie Todd has been trying to obtain a second superintendency for 4 years. She's completing her ninth year as superintendent of the Ennyburg Schools, a K-8 district of about 400 students. Her children are grown and off on their own, and she's willing to relocate to just about any part of the state.

Prior to securing the position at Ennyburg, she had been assistant superintendent in a mid-sized, suburban school district on the other side of the county. She occupied that position 4 years, after having been promoted from Language Arts and Social Studies Curriculum Coordinator. While her children were young, she taught in several different school districts for a total of 12 years, including 24 months of substitute teaching at all grade levels, and had two brief child-rearing leaves. In her current superintendency, there is only one other full-time administrator (the school business manager), so much of her work includes responsibilities that a typical building principal would have. She has a PhD in educational administration.

Marie's had numerous interviews for superintendencies during the past 4 years and has been among the top three semifinalists several times. "But I seem to keep coming up short. I'm not sure what it is," she says. "It's so hard to get any feedback other than, 'Things just didn't click with the board.' Or 'You weren't the best fit for the district.' You tell me what that's supposed to mean!"

Another applicant, Marlene Balsam, believes she knows what "fit" means in her own case. "It's a codeword. If there's not a real lot of brown faces among the schoolchildren in a district, I might as well not even apply. Look around the whole country. Where do you see administrators like me?"

Marlene is an African American woman with a distinguished school leadership career. After teaching for 6 years in an urban system in an adjoining state, she moved to the Capital City School District for her first elementary principalship. She spent 4 years in each of her subsequent positions in that district: a second elementary principalship, a middle school principalship, a high school principalship, and currently, one of four assistant superintendencies at the Capital City central office. Her reputation as an outstanding administrator meant that she was sent to whichever school or office seemed to need the most help. She enjoyed and thrived in each new role.

Marlene is being encouraged by one of her mentors to become a superintendent. Six months ago, she tried, unsuccessfully, for the Capital City superintendency. The person hired had more extensive experience than she did and, although she was disappointed, she understood the school board's decision. Now she feels she has limited options: "Let's be realistic. I can try for, perhaps, a half-dozen other superintendencies in this state, should they come open in the near future. Or I can leave here and go to another high minority, urban district in another part of the country. Do other candidates have to make that choice? Most would have 600, not six, other districts in this state alone they could go for, should the vacancy arise." In her view, skin color factors heavily into the hiring of school superintendents.

How do these women's concerns and experiences relate to superintendent search and selection processes? Is there discrimination, based on color and sex, that limits some candidates' prospects? If so, what are the strategies that can be employed to deal with such constraints? The goal of this chapter is to expose both overt and subtle biases that affect access to the superintendency.

Overt Discrimination and Bias

Radich's (1992) study found that "even in 1990, blatant discrimination against women in educational administration was . . . a part of the superintendent search process" (p. 183). Five years later, Grogan and Henry (1995) studied the relationship between school boards and women superintendent candidates. They found that "the superintendency continues to be constructed as a male arena" (p. 172). They conclude that a male-centered, "warrior, military, or business mentality" predominates in conceptions of the superintendency, to the disadvantage of female superintendent candidates (p. 172).

This study supports both Radich's (1992) and Grogan and Henry's (1995) findings about gender biases in superintendent selection. Among the most overt were expressions of negative preconceived expectations and prejudicial questions asked of or about women candidates in interview or screening situations. Representative of several consultants' remarks, a headhunter explains, "We occasionally run into the old mythologies: Can she do discipline? Can she do budget? Can she be tough enough to do whatever needs to be done? Can she do the job?" A school board member reports being asked by a member of their citizen screening team, "Is the problem you're having with this candidate because she has breasts?" His answer was "yes." He could not envision a woman being up to the demands and challenges of the superintendency.

A female candidate who interviewed for but was not offered a particular superintendency shares this experience: "The board president said to me twice, 'I was such good friends with Harry [the former superintendent]. Harry and I used to go out after board meetings and have a drink. We were very close. We did a lot of things together.' I'm thinking, okay, I know darn well we're not going to be going out for drinks together! So is he trying to tell me that that's the expectation? I'm thinking, Why is he telling me this? Why is he saying this? Where does a woman fit into his scheme of things then? It was a seven-member board, with four men and three women."

In a not-so-subtle way, this board president is communicating a set of gender-stereotypical expectations that would be virtually impossible for her, or any other female candidate, to meet. She, in fact, could not fit into his scheme of things—what some would call his operant "mental models."

Other consultants recount gendered inquiries from board members such as, "You know, what the hell does she know about a damn school bus if it breaks down?" Even when satisfactory affirmative responses emerge from such inquiries and females advance among the semifinalists, another level of bias can appear. A school board member admits, "Sure, gender biases still exist on boards. Even when the woman candidate becomes a finalist, then the question becomes, Do we have to pay her as much as the male contender?"

Numerous examples relate to headhunters reminding board members about nonsexist language: the new superintendent, he or she. Sometimes, sexist language appears even when intended as support of a female candidate. To wit, another consultant reports, "Three times in the interview this one gentleman on the board could be heard saying, 'That's my kinda girl!' He was just incorrigible." Although this board member's intent was encouragement and praise, he was unaware that his choice of language could be interpreted as paternalistic or demeaning to women.

Some consultants who sit in on board interviews with semifinalists underscore the difficulty of preventing board members from asking illegal or inappropriate questions, even with diligent prior training. A woman headhunter points out that board members are equally curious about potentially discriminatory factors that affect both male and female candidates: inquiries about marital status, age, and children. Another consultant alludes to the depth and breadth of gender biases, even in the preliminary stages of organizing a search: "Normally, when I sit down with a board, if the board has anything to say about gender, it comes across as if it's almost axiomatic that we're going to hire a male, who is going to be married, and who is going to have kids. He's going to live in the community, and the kids are going to attend the schools. So they have this stereotypic notion about what that candidate will look like."

This observation echoes findings from research conducted by Bell (1988) more than 10 years earlier. In her words, "The expectations . . . of superintendents are likely to be based on a taken-for-granted conception of the superintendent as a middle-aged, conservative, married man (Bell, 1988, p. 42). Again, what appear to be operating are traditional mental models, born out of historical and personal experience with primarily white, married men occupying positions of leadership. These models reflect an enduring cultural preference for male leaders in American society (Dunlap & Schmuck, 1995; Kanter, 1977; Marshall, 1997).

Gender stereotypes and employment. Informants for this study point to other gender-stereotypical and unfair preferences in hiring as well. For example, in a school board member's explanation of why a female semifinalist didn't get the job, "The discussion was that, well, this guy, the successful hire, had lost his job and had a family to support. And she has a husband. That was actually publicly discussed!" Clearly, overt gender discrimination is at work in this instance. Moreover, 65% of school board members interviewed in Radich's (1992) study indicated that gender was a discussion item at some point in their superintendent selection process.

Sometimes, the precedent set by other female administrators in the district can affect the superintendent hiring decision. For example, a consultant recounts: "In my last search, the board set out with a notion, on the part of several board members, that they would really like a woman superintendent. They already had other women administrators in their schools, and their experience had been that they would have someone who worked twice as hard, because you have to work twice as hard to get that far if you were a woman. That's a rough paraphrase, but they actually said that." In this case, the female candidate's sex worked in her favor, by association with other high-performing women administrators.

At other times, the presence of female administrators in a district can work against female candidates for the superintendency. A consultant shares how one board's discussion went: "My God, we've got a woman running the high school, and we already have an elementary principal who is a woman. Why are we even considering hiring another woman?" My follow-up question to that information was, Have you ever heard a board discuss similar concerns about male candidates in any of your searches? The answer was no. It is highly unlikely that such a question would be raised about prospective superintendents who are men. White male applicants and incumbents are the norm; females and nonwhites are the "others" (Chase, 1995; Chase & Bell, 1990; Ortiz & Marshall, 1995; Ortiz & Ortiz, 1995).

There were also illustrations of biases associated with gender that are more specific (e.g., related to single motherhood). A successful candidate's story is illustrative: "When I was leaving my first superintendency, one of the board members said to me, 'I want you to know how sorry I am to see you go. You've done a wonderful job, and I've loved everything you've done. But I have to tell you, I didn't vote for you when we appointed you. I didn't think a single mother could take on the responsibilities of this job and do it well. But you've proved me wrong.'"

This example suggests that, in the absence of similar role models in the past, leaders who are "others" face extraordinary expectations for proving themselves. This is similar to the kinds of discrimination Kanter (1977) found in the corporate world, when token representation, rather than a critical mass of females, characterized executive leadership.

Another quite specific form of bias relates to divorced and single candidates. As a board member elaborates on her extensive network among other board members across the state, she reveals, "You can't ask about marital status in the interview, but that's the type of thing you can find out from board member to board member. You can find that out." I asked why it's important to find out. She continued, "Some boards don't want a divorced person, because of the board's values. They want married with children. And not single." Again, I inquired, Why? "Because of traditional values. Images for the community. Is there a family unit there? Can they make a marriage work?"

Perhaps not surprisingly, I was unable to locate any research that finds a correlation between the ability to make a marriage work and effectiveness in the superintendency. Nevertheless, other board members, consultants, and researchers confirm that marriage and offspring are often interpreted as proxies for traditional family values, stability, and other virtues expected of school superintendents (Tyack & Hansot, 1982). For example, a veteran, male board member, whose term included having hired four different superintendents, explains, "You're always looking for a stable background. Someone who isn't on his or her fourth marriage."

Hmmmm. His or her. At first blush, this may seem like a discriminatory employment filter that affects males and females equally. The reality is, however, that it disproportionately affects women. How so? Because we know that in the general population, higher percentages of women (10.5%) than men (8.4%) are divorced; higher proportions of men (62.1%) than women (58.6%) are married (U.S. Bureau of the Census, 1997). Also, more women than men in the general population are single parents. Additionally, previous studies specific to superintendents show that men are more likely than women to be married with children; women are more likely than men to be divorced or single (Glass, 1992; O'Connell & Tallerico, 1998).

These data on gender and marital status are also of interest with respect to the tradition of including the semifinalists' spouses in the dinner meetings associated with superintendent selection processes. Although some boards and consultants no longer follow this practice, about two thirds of the participants in this study indicate that this tradition persists. It remains unclear whether or to what degree single and divorced candidates are disadvantaged by their solo participation in such dinners. It does seem, however, that the value of this practice warrants questioning. A candidate in this study connected this potential bias to larger, cultural traditions in our country: "It's like, could a bachelor or a single woman run for president or governor? I'm not sure. I think that Americans create certain expectations of their leaders. I think it's a cultural thing."

Consultants' part. Of all of the illustrations of gender bias and discrimination in this study, however, some of the most powerful findings were the cases where board members reported being asked by their consultant, Is this district ready for a woman? Is this board ready for a female superintendent? These questions are blatantly biased in and of themselves, as well as potentially prejudicial to the entire search and selection process.

They are particularly powerful by virtue of their having been raised by the professionals specifically selected for the expertise and objectivity they could bring to these processes. Such questions harken back to findings from a study that some colleagues and I conducted 5 years prior to this one and that had inspired our interest in learning more about headhunting practices (Tallerico & Burstyn, 1996; Tallerico, Burstyn, & Poole, 1993; Tallerico, Poole, & Burstyn, 1994). In that research, one of our female superintendent informants recounts this experience:

> There had been 150 applicants and the consultant, I think this is interesting, picked 10 for [the board's] review. I was not among the 10. And one of the school board members asked the consultant, "Wasn't there anyone who applied who had a good background in curriculum and instruction?" And [the consultant] said, "Yes, but I don't think you people are ready for a woman." But the board decided they wanted to see me. . . . Isn't this interesting? I didn't know this 'til much later. The school board member who asked that question . . . told me this later. (Tallerico & Burstyn, 1996, p. 660)

Other researchers' findings corroborate the existence of administrative powerbrokers' gender-biased assessments of certain districts' "readiness" for women superintendents (Skrla, 1998). These preconceptions reflect assumptions that school boards and district communities are routinely ready for male educational leaders, whereas the possibilities for women's acceptance are questionable, exceptional, or unnatural.

Strategies for female candidates. Such gender-biased assumptions are not surprising to experienced women administrators who apply for superintendencies. Many have developed ways of handling overt prejudices and confronting gender stereotyping in search and selection processes. For example, in an open forum for community members, one candidate successfully redirects an audience member's gendered concern as follows:

"A man in the crowd stands up and informs me, 'This is a football town and you're a woman. What are we going to do with that?' At first, I couldn't help laughing out loud. Then I turned it around and said, 'Well, I do know about football. But I think that what you're looking for is a leader, and you really don't care whether it's male or female. Isn't that right? Isn't that what you want, a really good leader?'" Here, she turns a sexist assumption into an additional opportunity for her to proceed to reinforce her own leadership prowess. There may be times when it will be fruitful for you to do the same.

Other candidates underscore the importance of anticipating the unasked questions about which they know boards and communities are curious but may avoid broaching. A candidate seeking her first superintendency explains, "I was almost through with an interview, and no one had mentioned anything about my lack of superintendent experience. I knew it was something they'd talk about after I left. It's an issue many women face. So I brought it up. I laid everything out on the table and showed them how my other experiences prepared me for the job and why I'd be such a good fit for their district."

Similar strategies can be used to preempt gender-stereotypical concerns about other, more specific competencies as well. An informant explains, "For women, the financial piece is very important. Because it's often perceived that we don't know anything about that. It's been important for me not to be intimidated by that. When the board hasn't brought it up, I have. I give examples, and I'm very clear about what I know. Sometimes, the interviewers don't bring up those things because they assume you wouldn't know about it anyway."

Often, the unasked questions include illegal topics mentioned earlier. In this study, some women candidates thought it wise to introduce those issues themselves: "I know they wonder about, Am I married? Do I have kids? Do I live a conservative life, or are they going to see me out Friday nights dancing at the local club? So I get all of that right out in the open, address those things without them asking, and use it as an opportunity to provide more information about the kind of person I am and what I will bring to the job." Another candidate who also opts for openness reports, "I know they can't ask those questions about family status, so I bring it up. I just say, 'I'm a divorced, single parent. I'm real proud of my kids and how I've raised them. And because they're all grown now, I have a lot of time to devote to the job.' I get it out and get it over with, so they're not left wondering."

The downside of these choices. These strategies, however, introduce the possibility of several negative consequences. For example, such directness may potentially offend, exacerbate the prejudice, or remove the candidate from further consideration. Clearly, most of the women in this study assess the benefits to outweigh the costs or risks involved, particularly with respect to personal matters of background, marital status, children, divorce, and other areas of inquiry precluded by law. Thus, this research reveals that the privacy and nondisclosure laws created to prevent discriminatory employment inquiries are commonly circumvented by both applicants and employers alike.

These examples demonstrate that many candidates believe that their interests are better served by self-disclosing and controlling the delivery and contextualization of this personal information themselves. They have learned that their silence on these issues can disadvantage them. Individuals chip away independently at obstacles that may stand in the way of the superintendency.

But beyond the individual, what are the consequences of such practices for the common good? What are the collective costs to the groups such laws are intended to protect? What about the broader social value of equitable employment opportunities regardless of personal background? Legal protections of privacy become more and more hollow each time candidates, board members, and headhunters reinterpret or circumvent them. In this way, for example, candidates' confrontation of gender biases in interviews may appear to be proactive and beneficial to their advancement to the superintendency. But on another level, such actions may also be understood as collusion with, and reproduction of, systemic inequities and injustices (Chase, 1995; Chase & Bell, 1990; Ferguson, 1984; Van Nostrand, 1993).

Self-interest and/or broader community citizenship with social justice? You will need to decide for yourself, to strike a balance with which you can live. Chase and Bell's research underscores this challenge. "Isolated struggle against inequality is the requirement and cost of professional success" for female superintendents (Chase, 1995, p. 33). Yet "individual actions do not change the systems that produce the constraints" (Chase & Bell, 1990, p. 172).

The Special Case of Special Groups

You may also need to make choices about the kinds of formal and informal support groups with which you affiliate. A particular kind of risk seems to be relevant to females' choices to participate, or not, in professional associations geared to women's concerns, in organizations that advocate for gender equity, or in particular conferences or workshop sessions designed to help nontraditional candidates advance in educational administration.

In this study, candidates' perspectives on this issue are wide ranging. Some underscore the value of seeking, developing, and participating in professional connections of all sorts, including both the administrative organizations and activities predominated by men, and those dedicated to the advancement of women and predominated by females.

Similar to the findings of Marshall (1985), Bell (1995), and Bell and Chase (1996), some participants in this study intentionally dissociate themselves from "women's groups" of any kind. A woman headhunter and former superintendent observes, "There seems to be some fear or anxiety to identify yourself as in a women's group when you're an administrator. I don't know why. When I was a superintendent, I would get together with four or five other women superintendents for a weekend two or three times a year. It was like a 'shadow' organization because no one except me wanted to get more aggressive and acknowledge the group."

A candidate explains why she avoids membership in women's groups this way: "The best thing for women superintendents is to just fit in with the others [male superintendents]. Because sometimes those separate groups are perceived in less than positive ways. At the [state superintendents' association conferences], I hear the guys joking about what's going on at the all-women's breakfast. It raises suspicions unnecessarily."

A male search consultant draws a connection between the conservative norms of school administration in general and the avoidance of all-female associations: "Many women superintendents have adopted different behaviors that they think will make them successful. And one of the behaviors is not to be associated with anything potentially controversial, or anything that could potentially be viewed as separatist in nature."

People of color face parallel choices in these regards. Some candidates praise the value, for example, of various black educators' organizations and informal support groups of African American administrators. Others voice concern about the risks of association with separate or single-race groups. A candidate recounts that "For years, I got together with a group of other African American administrators in the district. We always tried to help and support each other. There weren't that many of us. But we kept it quiet. It's like when some people see a group of black teenagers in the mall, they immediately get worried about what might occur. We knew better than to advertise what we were doing because that might make some people nervous."

With respect to their integration into the highest levels of educational administration, both females and people of color may be considered to occupy lower status groups than do Caucasian males. Ashforth and Mael's (1989) research on social identity suggests that those who belong to lower status groups may sometimes distance themselves from their own group to psychologically join a higher status group. This may explain the choices made by some women and people of color to dissociate themselves from single-sex or race-based support groups. Kanter (1977) identified this as a strategy sometimes used by token females in male-dominated leadership roles. Marshall (1985) found that "disidentifying with women" (p. 132) was one of several ways that female school administrators manage impressions of their "stigma" (p. 146) in a male-dominated field.

This issue of special group affiliations is an example of a subtler form of bias that may affect you as a potential future applicant for the superintendency. How so? Because these are choices and consequences that most white male educators do not face (Bell, 1995; Bell & Chase, 1996). The question would likely never be raised, "Why is he a part of that white male group or association?" These are stigmas that apply exclusively to members of historically underrepresented groups.

You should know, however, that none of the African American or female informants for this study suggested that such specialized organizations take the place of their involvement in the conventional, administrator organizations that are a long-standing part of the profession. Rather, these more specialized associations are seen as supplements to those traditional support and development groups. Nevertheless, for women and people of color, these "different" kinds of affiliations are sometimes risky, in much the same way as are digressions from the preferred administrative career path to the superintendency.

Interviews as Subtler Forms of Bias

Prior research reveals that the interviews associated with employment selection are key venues for the enactment of several subtle forms of bias that also disadvantage women and people of color (Berman, 1997; Dipboye, 1992; Webb, Montello, & Norton, 1994; Wheatley, 1981). This is true in superintendent search and selection as well.

In this study, candidates, headhunters, and school board members confirm two major points about candidate interviews. First, interviews are a significant part of the weeding-out process. As one school board member summarizes, "They make or break candidates." Other board members, consultants, and candidates routinely refer to interviews as "critical," "key," and "crucial."

Second, it is in the interview setting where numerous intangibles come into play (Carter et al., 1993; Cullen, 1995). These intangibles are often described as the "chemistry" between the board and the applicant (during the final interviews and informal/dinner meetings), or between the consultant and the applicant (during their conversations prior to being referred to the school board). These intangibles are also a part of the board's and consultant's judgment of the fit between the candidate and the community. More specifically, these are value filters, often expressed in terms like the following: "Things really 'clicked' [or didn't] between us"; "It was more of a 'gut feel' than anything else"; "It's sort of an undefinable thing"; or "I could just tell we were [or weren't] on the same wavelength."

Like the mental models of appropriate career paths mentioned earlier, these intangibles have to do with whom we can picture in the specific leadership context of the superintendency. And, who we can picture often has a great deal to do with who we have previously seen in leadership positions, whether school administrators, government officials, or chief executive officers of Fortune 500 companies (Ferguson, 1984; Kanter, 1977).

In the interview setting, however, additional, subtler factors also come into play. According to this study's participants, assessments of "positive" chemistry and "good" fit are strongly related to how comfortable board members feel interacting with the candidate in their respective authority roles. As a consultant explains, "It really comes down to what kinds of personalities can get along." Another headhunter reiterates, "When all is said and done, the board decides on the basis of personality and chemistry. They get by the concern about qualifications, because they assume that all the finalists are very competent. So they put all that aside and concentrate on looking for the person they want to interact with on a daily basis." Will the interactions feel natural or awkward? Relaxed or strained? Another consultant explains, "If the board likes the person and they find they're relating well in the interview, that tends to carry the day."

Board members' explanations corroborate headhunters' depictions of the power of these interpersonal intangibles of liking, relating well to, and feeling comfortable with. This board member's comments are illustrative of many others' comments: "Of all the candidates you see, you're trying to figure out, Who will I be able to work with? Who will I be able to just pick up the phone and call? Who am I most at ease with?" Another board member reports, "At the point of the interview, it's personal chemistry. It's what we like, what we see, what we hear, how we feel about the person. No matter anything else."

Other salient intangibles have to do with appearance. On one hand, virtually all boards want excellent communicators who are masters at interacting with savvy stakeholders, state legislators, education commissioners, businesspeople, teachers, and the media (Carter & Cunningham, 1997; Kowalski, 1995; Norton, Webb, Dlugosh, & Sybouts, 1996). On the other hand, fitting in with the local community often invokes subtle expectations relevant to socioeconomic status and class.

The following examples from board members are telling: "The hire must match your community. There must be a fit. We didn't hire one candidate who was an excellent scholar because he talked down to us. We thought he would similarly talk down to our teachers. Another time, we didn't hire a candidate who was too much of a hick for our community. We may be small and upstate, but not like that. But a 'Mr. Personality' can be overdone, too, and our board has been turned off by that, too. You can't be too flashy in this community."

As another school board member describes the influence of appearance and social status fit: "Each board has a personality. If you can feel or get to know that personality, you can get a feel for the fit with the people you're interviewing. For example, if it's a serious, intellectual, bright board, you really need someone smart. If it's a rural, blue-collar board, you don't want to bring them in sophisticated persons who are really slickly dressed and not of that same background because that will really turn off a rural community. You don't want somebody who looks a lot richer than the school board members."

Why is this bias? On one level, these intuitions about appearance and fit affect all interviewees, but nonwhite candidates are at a particular disadvantage if skin color "match" with either school board members or communities is a part of the unstated (or unconscious) appearance criteria. We know, for example, that just 4.9% of school board members are African American, 2% Hispanic, 0.7% Asian American, and 0.1% American Indian ("Education Vital Signs," 1997). Additionally, subtle cross-cultural understandings may be an invisible part of the chemistry that either works or doesn't work for the cultural-majority interviewers who hold most of the keys to accessing the superintendency.

With respect to sex, some board members and consultants relate more stringent standards for women's appearance. The following remarks from a veteran board member illustrate this well.

I think women applicants have to be really careful about dress. Besides the conservative interview suits—because both women and men should wear those—I hear the women criticized for the makeup, the size of the purse, the accessories, the hairdo, how much grey is in her hair, the height of the heels, the length of the skirt, the color of the fingernails. We even had a woman candidate wear diamond earrings! Diamond earrings are completely inappropriate!

Many of the variables mentioned in this quote suggest appearance disqualifiers unique to women and largely inapplicable to male candidates. Similarly, because appearance and age are often closely interrelated, the tacit age biases that disproportionately affect women (discussed earlier) can be reinforced in the interview setting.

Moreover, if previous research about men's and women's communication patterns holds true, the intangibles of with whom board members and consultants are on the same wavelength and to whom they relate more comfortably also tip the scales in the direction of male candidates. Tannen's (1990) studies, for example, show how differences in men's and women's learned communication styles can result in "culture clashes" and misunderstandings between the sexes. This communicative compatibility becomes significant in board and consultant interview settings wherein men are usually in the majority, as well as in the positions of power.

Bell's (1988) findings about factors that boards use in superintendent selection confirm that "the most persuasive characteristic a candidate for superintendent could possess seems to be maleness. . . . Maleness signifies to board members . . . shared language and experience, predictability, connection with the power structure, and leadership that satisfies stereotyped preferences" (p. 50). Linn's (1998) research on educational selection decisions concludes that "even well-meaning decision makers often subtly advantage people like themselves" (p. 16).

Supporting earlier research on superintendent search and selection (Rickabaugh, 1986; Wrubel, 1990), this study found that it is through these interview intangibles that some of the greatest disconnects from the stated priorities and qualifications agreed upon at the start of the process occur. It is here that, despite the consultant's and others' best efforts to keep the decision making objective and focused on the standards, quality indicators, and criteria on which they had taken great pains to arrive at consensus when the search was initiated, the process becomes intuitive and unpredictable—that is, human and biased.

As an experienced headhunter explains, "I'd like to tell you that there's a really scientific way of doing all this. Then you'd feel a lot better. [Laugh.] But there are no absolutes to it." This assessment was echoed by virtually all of the informants for this study. Put another way, by a different consultant:

> Let's face it, there's nothing scientific about a search for a superintendent and the process. You try to structure the process, you try to gather information, you try to develop criteria, you try to

set standards, assess whatever information you have against those standards. But it's still a very nonobjective process. You're dealing with people's personal tastes. I think of it as art, rather than science.

In the words of another headhunter, "Every interview is a subjective as well as an objective process. The objective part is when you structure the interview questions and ask every candidate the same questions. The subjective piece is that you're also trying to find out who the person is as a person. That's where gut feelings about integrity, honesty, candor, and fit come in." (Simultaneously, of course, the candidates themselves are also trying to assess those intangibles: how well they are "clicking" with board members, and how great the potential is for the match to endure.)

An important piece to keep in mind, however, is that the first, and most numerous, chemistry matches are made long before the school board sees any candidates. In the initial paper screening, and the consultant interviews and reference checks, headhunters make their judgments about advancing or eliminating applicants based on their individual assessments of personality, style, and status fits with the hiring board and community. As a consultant explains, "I design a personalized scoring chart when I review files and applicants. I include the 8 to 10 criteria the board developed, then I add some criteria of my own. Some are nitty-gritty things like administrative certifications. But I also include my gut feeling about the match with this board. I get a sense of the chemistry, and I rank that too." Another headhunter reflects, "Once you get into those perceptions about style and fit, you get further and further away from the profile that was set out. There's a lot of wiggle room there, and we all participate in it."

So what? These examples illustrate a number of points. First, they show how this admittedly fuzzy criterion of "chemistry/personality" is a part of selection right from the start of the process. Second, they demonstrate the ability of consultants to introduce additional screening criteria into the process, beyond what the board may specify. Third, they underscore the power of the consultant's personal judgment of the already subjective, unwritten, personality/fit criteria.

My purpose in emphasizing these factors is not to lament the unscientific or nonobjective parts of employment decision making. Like all human endeavors, superintendent selection will be subjective.

Nor am I suggesting that all assessment criteria must be written, because that's an equally impossible standard to implement.

Instead, this discussion aims to reveal how these subjectivities are more likely to favor male rather than female, majority rather than minority, candidates. The disconnects with the stated qualifications, coupled with the predominance of gut feelings, chemistry, and intuition, allow personal and cultural biases to wield significant influence at key decision points. Such biases (often subconscious or unconscious) are more likely to disadvantage women and people of color, because it is they who are the "others" in relation to the primarily white, male headhunters and school board members who make the screening decisions.

These analyses are supported by both social-psychological and organizational research that demonstrates a human affinity for interaction with those most like ourselves. (Remember, many of the characterizations of intuition and gut proffered by this study's informants center on feelings of comfort with and ability to relate to the interviewees.)

For example, Byrne's (1971) studies reveal that demographic similarity on characteristics like sex, race, and age leads to perceived similarity in attitudes and values, which leads to interpersonal attraction. Kanter (1977) found that because demographic similarity generates interpersonal attraction, many organizations engage in what is called "homosocial reproduction." In other words, individuals tend to like and promote those most like themselves. Particular to the superintendency, Bell (1988) points out that because "trustworthiness and predictability are [usually] signified by social homogeneity" (p. 56), "the woman superintendent's gender is interpreted as a symbol of overriding difference and risk" (p. 55). This influences superintendent selection, as well as on-the-job superintendent-school board relations.

Summary and Implications

What and where are the biases that affect access to the superintendency? As this chapter demonstrates, gender and cultural stereotypes, biased expectations, and prejudices appear in many different forms. Overt biases can negatively influence every stage of the process, from preliminary discussions about the search (e.g., Is this district ready for a woman superintendent?), through finalists' interviews (e.g., What does she know about athletics or transportation?), to appointment (e.g., Do we have to pay her as much as a man?)

On a personal note, I was surprised by the specific examples that this study's informants shared that are blatantly discriminatory or overtly biased. The surprise had to do with two different dimensions; first, sheer frequency. Illustrations were numerous and varied; I reported only selected examples in this chapter. Second, the illustrations did not come only from nontraditional or unsuccessful candidates, but, rather, from headhunters, school board members, and successful candidates of all backgrounds. There was broad distribution of examples, irrespective of informants' roles or district context.

This chapter also exposed more subtle and indirect filters that disadvantage females and candidates of color. These included, for example, tacit assumptions about the undesirability of candidates who are divorced, unmarried, or single parents (e.g., females outnumber males in each of these groups in the general population); and hypervaluing of interpersonal chemistry in screening interviews (which fosters the introduction of subconscious preferences for affiliation with those most like ourselves).

The latter is particularly significant in that nonminority males predominate in each of the roles key to candidate advancement. That is, most headhunters are white men. Most people with the authority to hire superintendents (school board members) are white men. Most of the key sources of reference checks valued most highly by headhunters and school board members are white men.

Taken together, both the broader, cultural conditions that support the leadership of nonminority males in American society (see Chapter 4) and the overt and covert biases particular to superintendent search and selection practices present women and people of color with challenges, concerns, barriers, and ambiguities that most white male candidates for superintendencies do not have to face.

This chapter has identified several strategies that some female and minority candidates use to deal with potentially discriminatory circumstances. These include anticipating and preempting biased inquiries by introducing information about personal background and marital status themselves, employing humor to turn around sexist and racist remarks, and deflecting inappropriate comments by changing the subject to focus on positive personal attributes and skills. The limitations of these approaches were discussed in terms of the tension between advancing one's own cause and contributing to the perpetuation of unfair and inequitable employment practices.

6

How Do Consultants and School Boards Help?

Delores Sage, consultant, has been assisting school districts for 10 years. Superintendent search and selection is one of several services that her firm provides, along with school board development, program evaluation, and diversity awareness training. She typically works on a three-person team made up of a Hispanic female former assistant superintendent; a European American male professor of educational administration; and herself, an African American former superintendent.

Sage's firm markets its search services by advertising its record of, and reputation for, aggressively recruiting and placing members of historically underrepresented groups in the superintendency. Delores attributes the firm's success to its wide network of contacts with females and people of color in educational leadership positions throughout the United States: "When we ask these persons for nominations, we can count on their not giving us an exclusively male or white list." Also, Sage keeps in close contact with the executive directors of state and national associations of women, African American, and Hispanic educators, using them as resources and reference checks.

Delores and her teammates frequently speak at conferences for aspiring administrators, and they make as many guest appearances as they can at colleges and universities that offer educational administrator preparation degrees. They take a long-term, developmental view of cultivating interest in the superintendency by nurturing the various pipelines of potential school leaders in the early stages of their careers. They often provide individual coaching on interview skills for women and minorities who seek their assistance.

What are some of the practices that allow nontraditional candidates broader access to the superintendency? What actions help to remove barriers and widen, rather than narrow, the pathways to this important educational leadership role?

Despite the gender and racial biases underscored in the previous chapter, there is also evidence that some headhunters, school board members, and candidates are doing much to reject limited constructions of the superintendency as an exclusively Caucasian male domain (Kamler, 1995; Kamler & Shakeshaft, 1998; Maienza, 1986; Radich, 1992). They are raising questions, challenging norms, and removing historic obstacles in order to open up superintendent search and selection processes to a diverse range of candidates. These promising practices are the subject of this chapter.

Equity and Diversity Values

Some search consultants and school board members value gender, racial, and ethnic diversity, and they honor that commitment in their superintendent search and selection practices. This value is sometimes expressed in terms of recognizing the contributions that members of historically marginalized groups can make to leadership. For example, a school board member explains, "I think whites have a lot to learn from African American leaders, just as much as the reverse. And that's valuable, in the superintendency and everywhere else. It's good for all our children to see that." Relatedly, a search consultant emphasizes that "Sometimes, women can bring something new and different to the role. Many don't want to act like the men superintendents who went before them. Women have to be themselves, and, of course, they can have unique strengths to bring to school administration."

Candidates corroborate that consultants are opening doors for women, consistent with values of gender fairness. An applicant remarks, "I can see that [some consultants] are trying to promote diversity. They're really making a concerted effort to change some of the hiring behaviors and make the pool much more diverse. It's on their agenda to do that, and I hear that women across the state are feeling it. Philosophically, they think that a much more diverse population should be presented to boards." Kamler's (1995) study supports these candidates' observations. She found that search consultants included a higher percentage of females in the slate of semifinalists that they forwarded to school boards than there was in their original pools of applicants.

At other times, valuing gender and racial diversity can mean actively countering some of the stereotypes that disadvantage women, such as viewing femaleness as oppositional to administrative competency. When one of this study's consultants hears such references to gender biases, he points out, "It would be absurd and arrogant to believe that 50% of the population doesn't have leadership potential. That just doesn't make sense, and it cuts too many people out of the process." Another search consultant acknowledges the gender biases that exist in school leadership and tries to turn that around to benefit the female candidates she brings to boards; she frequently suggests, "They have to work twice as hard to get this far if they are women in this field, so please know these are very hard-working administrative applicants."

Honoring values of equity and diversity can also mean simply starting with the assumption that this particular board and community is "ready for" a qualified superintendent of either gender or any cultural background. Rather than questioning such readiness, some headhunters' language serves to continually reinforce openness to multiple possibilities regarding the top candidates: "He or she may become finalists," and "His or her final visits to the community will be the last week of April."

Developing Pipelines

These diversity-affirming values are often accompanied by a long-term perspective on leadership development for the schools. That is, it is recognized that diversity in the chief executive position is contingent upon greater heterogeneity in earlier leadership roles. The experience of a headhunter who recently helped place three African American males and seven Caucasian females in superintendencies illustrates this point:

> We've been able to make some real inroads though the searches we've done. The last seven or eight candidates placed have not

looked at all like what I looked like [white, male] when I went into the superintendency. And that hasn't happened just because it would happen naturally. It happened because some people around here have been very thoughtful about developing talent and have been encouraging people over the years to consider new things in administration.

Such advocacy often drives an interest in decreasing the long-standing relative homogeneity of key positions that have historically served as stepping stones to the superintendency (e.g., high school principalships and assistant superintendencies). To this end, school boards and headhunters who prize gender, ethnic, and racial diversity in the superintendency engage in practices that help build heterogeneity from the bottom up.

What does this attention to potential pipelines look like? It can involve encouraging women and teachers of color to complete administrative licensure programs and to acquire broader leadership skills through experiences on building- or districtwide planning and decision-making teams, or through roles such as assistant principalships, staff development, and program coordination. A number of consultants use their adjunct or other teaching in administrator preparation programs at colleges and universities as vehicles for identifying and encouraging nontraditional prospective candidates to consider the superintendency. Some are proactive about maintaining connections to those students and following their careers for years after the initial coursework contact ends.

In this way, attending to potential supply pipelines also includes encouraging women and people of color who have acquired foundational leadership skills and accomplishments to experience wider leadership responsibilities and increased political, financial, and communications challenges. As a consultant describes this long-term advocacy, "Hopefully, I'll be able to help get those people into some leadership roles where they'll be real contributors."

Some consultants see leadership recognition and development as part of their job. Some also make certain that women and minority group members receive particular attention. As one explains, "Part of our job is to promote, both literally and figuratively, talent. And that means all kinds of people, not just men or Caucasians. I tap the entire talent pool. And it's not only seeking talent when there's a vacancy, but to encourage talent whenever and wherever we see it. That helps everyone in the long run." Again, this often involves pointing women and minority prospective candidates in the direction of administrative openings and expressing confidence in their ability to excel in new roles and venues.

These findings support those from Hudson's (1994) study of access to the superintendency. She found that minority superintendents (i.e., females and Blacks) were more likely than majority superintendents (White males) to use informal sources to learn about job openings. Those informal sources included other superintendents, school board members, professional acquaintances, and college professors.

Maienza (1986) found that women candidates for the superintendency were frequently sponsored by "consultants to whom they [had] become visible by virtue of their extraordinary activity within their own districts and across districts" (p. 70). Bell and Chase (1996) also found that women superintendents' positive professional connections to White men helped them become integrated into the power structures and support networks of educational administration that lead to superintendencies.

In this study, time and again candidates confirmed the significance of these kinds of connections throughout their careers. An African American woman relates that, "I've had encouragement from three different search consultants who said either 'Try this next,' or 'Someday, you're going to be a superintendent.' They dropped information to me and got me thinking about next steps. It's clear to me that that's their expectation. And it eventually became my own expectation."

An example from another woman illustrates how headhunters' positive expectations and confidence can inspire candidates to set their sights higher than they might have otherwise. In this case, "higher" meant more affluent, suburban districts: "I started to target these kinds of districts only because [consultant] encouraged me to. He said, 'You really can do it. Don't be intimidated by it and don't think you can't. Even though you're coming from a rural superintendency, I know you can be successful here too. There's no reason why you can't be, if you want to.'" In this instance, the candidate and consultant had come to know each other during a previous search in which the candidate was not offered the superintendency. This consultant exhibits both a long-term perspective on talent development for superintendency pools and an advocacy role in promoting non-traditional candidates.

Recruiting Affirmatively

Besides these kinds of alliances and encouragement to promote diversity throughout multiple levels of the educational leadership and administrative pipelines, some school board members and head-hunters actively recruit qualified women (Kamler, 1995) and people of color for particular superintendency vacancies. Sometimes, this involves calling or writing individual candidates directly. An African American board member explains that she "silently recruited" women and African American candidates for each of the three superintendent searches in which she was involved. This meant making confidential calls to experienced administrators with outstanding reputations in the area and encouraging them to apply to her district.

Many female candidates in this study confirmed being invited to apply in parallel, gender-related circumstances: "[Consultant] called me and said to me he was particularly interested in women candidates because he had a real interest in diversity. I was quite taken with his desire to recruit good candidates in that way. I applied for that superintendency." Similarly, another candidate reports that "in [school district], the board of education president called and asked if I would apply. She's someone I had worked with through Zonta, a professional women's organization, when I was an administrator in a nearby district."

In other cases, the promotion is more indirect, often a matter of influencing others (e.g., experienced administrators, other consultants) to initiate contacts with potential candidates. The following example from a female headhunter demonstrates this point: "I was at a conference and met a woman who, in half an hour, impressed me immensely. But she was from another part of the state. And I knew she would never come to my part of the state. So I told her that she needed to talk to [consultant]. And I called him and said, 'You need to talk to this woman for the search you're doing.' I know his interests are in quality and equity. He set up an interview with her, and he was as impressed with her as I was. He added her name to the other semi-finalists, and the board hired her." Similar illustrations showing how this powerful network can work for diversity surfaced repeatedly in this study.

Supporting Alliances

Sometimes, such promotion involves collaborating with specific advocacy networks, such as women administrators' or Black educators' professional organizations. This typically means intentionally targeting qualified nonwhite males, alerting them to currently available or prospective superintendency openings, and urging them to apply. As one consultant explains, "I was concerned that I was not getting African American candidates, so I called the president of the state association [of Black educators] and tried to get some help from them, on people who might want to be superintendents here. They were able to give me some names." Similarly, another headhunter speaks at as many regional meetings of the state women administrators' organization as he can, "really trying to drum up some candidates. I got two good applicants out of that group the last time I spoke there." These are examples of significant extra efforts to bring diversity to the slate of candidates to present to hiring school boards.

Acting affirmatively in this way carries with it all the hazards and potential conflicts of interest that direct targeting of majority culture candidates bears. Particularly problematic are the possibilities for candidates or other stakeholders to confuse encouragement to apply with promise of selection. Obviously, the latter is unfair and biased in itself. From many headhunters' perspectives, targeting of any applicants carries the chance of being perceived as bringing a stable of preferred candidates into a then-less-than-open search process. Board members who engage in active recruitment likewise run the risk of perceptions of stacking the deck.

The reality, however, is that recruitment of candidates goes on all the time behind the scenes, by consultants, school board members, teachers, incumbent administrators, citizens, mayors, and cousins twice removed. People learn of job openings. They tell others about them. They advocate for their preferred outcomes in the superintendent search and selection process. (See previous chapters.) The essential distinctiveness of acting affirmatively, however, is that targeting women and people of color ensures that white men will not be the only ones recruited. For the reasons discussed in Chapter 4 (e.g., the current hostile environment for affirmative action), consultants and school board members do not typically use this term to refer to their efforts to recruit a diverse pool of candidates.

Altering Common Procedures

In addition to the "broad brush" practices of valuing gender and ethnic/racial diversity, encouraging heterogeneity throughout leadership pipelines, and recruiting women and people of color for superintendent vacancies, there are numerous other ways in which headhunters and school boards design and execute their search and selection processes to mitigate prevailing gender and racial/ethnic biases.

One way is through the identification of the qualifications preferred of applicants, as articulated in written brochures or job advertisements and, more importantly, as understood in their selection and elimination processes. Boards and headhunters who wish to cast the net broadly for superintendency talent express (and enact) these qualifiers in terms of leadership skills and accomplishments, rather than specific previous positions held. A consultant explains, "It has to do with being good, about making a difference in the lives of kids and the culture of a school or district. It doesn't have to do with being a principal at a certain grade level. That's not how you or the board should be doing the screening."

Another consultant elaborates this point by underscoring the importance of keeping the ideal candidate profile centered on skills and qualities that have meaning for the superintendency: "To break those traditional barriers down, you have to insist, 'We're looking for someone with these skills. A high school principal is not a skill, it's an occupation. And how much time does a superintendent actually spend with high school issues? They spend time with the most severe discipline issues, in student hearings. But you don't have to have been a high school principal to do those. A school psychologist would do a better job at that than a high school principal."

Additionally, boards and search consultants interested in a diverse pool of superintendent candidates emphasize quality of prior experiences, rather than either narrow quantifiers of longevity or progression through a specific sequence of job titles. A headhunter emphasizes to boards, "Some applicants come with real long resumés and others with very short ones. But length of the resumé should not be a guiding factor in selection. Instead, we ought to be focusing on the quality of the experiences and the quality of the person as a leader." Because women are more likely than men to interrupt their educational careers for child rearing, the elimination of specific targets for minimal years in a particular role can help preclude their elimination from viable candidacy.

Another headhunter explains how he repeatedly reinforces a focus on leadership skills and potential, rather than particular job titles or number of years in administration: "When I do my screening, I demonstrate to the board how my screening is related to the leadership skills desired. When I do my interviewing, my questions are drawn directly from the skills criteria. When I help prepare them for the interviews, I show how the questions they will ask lead directly back to those skills and qualifications. So they begin to see that we're looking at the qualifications of people, not the positions they've held." Again, the reason such emphases help level the playing field for all candidates is that the highest proportions of women administrators and administrators of color are in staff (rather than line) leadership positions and elementary principalships, which are roles where they can acquire a broad range of leadership skills, even though these are not the positions from which superintendents have been drawn historically.

Thus, boards and headhunters interested in bringing increased gender and racial/ethnic heterogeneity to their superintendent candidate pools welcome applicants who have traveled unconventional pathways, provided they can demonstrate the desired educational leadership competencies. As one consultant put it, "Even though we know that a typical move is from the high school principalship to a superintendency, we also know that there are successful superintendents all across the United States with a range of backgrounds. I point that out to boards and screening committees. I excite them about candidates with alternative paths. That doesn't mean the person will get the job, but it does mean the person can get to the slate [of interviewees]."

A focus on leadership skills applicable to the superintendency from nontraditional roles can even extend to leveling the playing field for incumbent superintendents competing against other administrators in a given search. The following illustration comes from a consultant working to educate a school board about such possibilities. "There's often a clear favoritism towards experienced superintendents. Even if it wasn't a very good superintendency experience, some board members will say, 'Well, at least this person has been in the chair.' In many of those cases, I have argued, 'Well, is that really what you want to do? This person really hasn't got a very good track record as superintendent.' I try to move them to looking at the skills of the persons applying instead. What they have actually done and how well they have done it. I mean, the superintendency has certain generalizable leadership skills. And some are very transferable from other administrative experiences. So I try to get them to encourage some of those."

Another headhunter underscores the long-term benefit to women and minorities of such approaches: "Hopefully, whenever a candidate succeeds in a path that's nontraditional, what we're doing is building a new path for others in the future. It makes it credible, as a route, in the eyes of both the consultants and the boards."

The good news, according to this study's informants, is that such approaches do help to get more nontraditional candidates in front of boards and selection committees for interviews. However, consultants, board members, and candidates suggest that it is still the applicant whose career has followed the traditional rights of passage who is likely to be appointed to the superintendency. As one consultant summarizes, "All things being equal, if there are eight semifinalists and three of them have been principals and central office administrators, and the others are very skilled but haven't served in those positions, all things being equal, the more conventional path will be favored. There's a security in doing that."

Other strategies. What are some other practices employed by headhunters and school boards to foster broader access to the superintendency by members of historically underrepresented groups?

A few report using gender-mixed or racially mixed teams to screen the original pool of applications, rather than leaving this task to a single consultant. Several different reasons were provided for employing such a mix. For example, a female consultant believes that, "We're the ones who are often more sensitive to historic barriers."

Others point to the value of screening and interviewing as a mixed-sex team as a means to achieve greater objectivity in the process: "Three of us each review the paperwork independently, rate them independently, conduct the interviews together but then rate them independently, and then we sit down and talk about all of them. So if one of us has bad chemistry with a candidate, we can compensate for that by including the other two people in the discussion." Another consultant reports, "We explain to boards that this gender mix is by design. He and I knew that we could both be in the same candidate interview and hear different issues differently. So conducting interviews jointly allowed us a more comprehensive picture of each candidate." This rationale is supported by Tannen's (1990) research on men's and women's communication and relational styles; that, in fact, men and women do speak, hear, and listen for different signals in interpersonal dialogues.

Racially mixed screening teams seem to be employed less frequently than do gender-mixed teams. The former are used primarily when headhunters are working for mixed-race school boards, typically in urban districts. Rather than the modus operandi being a mixed-race consulting team, these headhunters contract on an ad hoc basis with people of color who are superintendents, professors, or board members to paper screen and/or interview candidates for a particular search. In contrast, when mixed-gender teams are used, it is often because that is the normal way for that consulting group/firm to operate. Nationally, there are relatively few consulting firms whose principals, and modus operandi, include people of color ("Meet the Powerbrokers," 1994).

Changing labels. Another strategy used by some headhunters and school boards is to delete candidates' names and substitute code numbers before sharing files with board or stakeholder selection committees. This practice can serve the dual purpose of protecting applicants' confidentiality and diminishing gender biases that may unconsciously affect the paper screening process. Often, however, candidates remain unprotected by this extra effort. Why? Because resumés highlight work locations, because it is easy to find information about other school districts and their personnel, and because many candidates do not venture far from their previous district when they apply for new superintendencies.

An additional strategy related to the organization and classification of written data can help women, minority, and other candidates who have not occupied the historically typical chairs in their careers—ensuring that the leadership skills, competencies, and qualities identified previously continue to serve as the categories of analysis as information throughout paper screening is collated and displayed by consultants and boards.

This procedure contrasts with the more commonplace practice of distinctions by particular previous positions. To illustrate this difference, a consultant explains, "After I've made the first cut of applicants myself, I bring the board about 20 applications to focus on. I intentionally avoid sorting those 20 by previous roles held. For example, in the last search I did, I brought them divided into three groups: the 10 best candidates applied to the board's qualifications criteria, the second-best matches with those criteria who are still good possibilities, and the ones who are not as good a match as the others in the first two groups." This technique demonstrates a way to begin to dislodge the career path templates that have been used in the past to sort and prioritize superintendent candidates.

Interviewing

The practices described in this chapter thus far center on what happens prior to becoming a semifinalist interviewee. Whereas virtually all boards participate in awareness-level training regarding illegal topics and questions to avoid, some headhunters work diligently to eliminate more subtle biases from candidate interviews. One way this is done is by sitting in as an observer and informal monitor of selection committees and board interviews. This affords the consultant the opportunity to intervene when, for example, a particular question is not raised in an interviewer's effort to spare a female candidate the anticipated embarrassment of addressing a technical question on facilities construction that she is presumed not to know. In this way, the consultant can monitor and correct both prejudicial omissions and more overt commissions of gender or other biases in the interview setting.

Other boards and consultants expend considerable effort to see as many semifinalists as possible face to face. Given the high impact of these interpersonal reactions in screening decisions, the goal here is to get the board and other interview committees to see more qualified people than is typical. This can increase the chances for women and other nontraditional candidates to present themselves directly to the people doing the hiring. As one consultant explains, "If you've got some people who are really outstanding in some regards, but don't meet all your criteria, I suggest to boards that they might want to hold a slot or two open for the nontraditional candidates, and then let the community and everybody else test them. Let's find out if the nontraditional candidates can show how their strengths match our criteria."

Other headhunters and board members advocate more directly. To wit, from a veteran board member, "If there's a candidate that looks to me like somebody worthy of further consideration, I may raise a few more questions if the board is moving in the direction of eliminating someone who I think has strong potential but might not be as traditional a candidate with some of the experiences."

Of course, seeing more semifinalists can mean expending more time. Some boards and headhunters have found ways to keep the total amount of time expended in the labor-intensive process of selecting a new superintendent at a reasonable level by eliminating extended dinner meetings with just two or three finalists, and instead conducting additional structured interviews with more than the usual six to eight semifinalists.

A consultant describes how this works, when coupled with the value of leadership diversity: "One of the things we changed was how the board invested its time in the search and selection process. They were able to see more semifinalists in their initial interviews by shortening them and making them more efficient. We also didn't do the going-to-dinner part, which can take four or five hours per candidate. That's only to provide a broader potential pool if you work with people to understand that they can't just look for a stereotypical candidate. Because otherwise bringing them into the screening process just means the board sees a lot more people, but they still end up with the same type candidates they always had: white males who are mid to late career."

As a side benefit, particularly to single and divorced candidates, the elimination of dinner meetings also means deleting spousal personality factors from entering the superintendent selection decision. This is consistent with the numerous examples throughout this chapter related to keeping the focus on candidates' past and potential leadership skills and contributions rather than extraneous, unnecessarily limiting, and potentially biasing variables (Berman, 1997; Webb et al., 1994).

Avoiding and Confronting Bias

Yet another strategy for getting more women and minority applicants in front of boards is for headhunters to ignore individual board members' expressed prejudices. As a consultant explains, "If a board says to me male over female, I simply ignore it. In my last search, if I had followed the board's indications, I would have not brought any women candidates to them. But I brought two women candidates out of six semifinalists to them. And those two candidates became the top two out of three in their selection."

Clearly, this practice carries risk for the consultant. Neglecting to attend to the employing board's stated preferences can translate into poor performance ratings that can harm the headhunter's reputation for delivering what boards want in the future.

Other board members and consultants deal with the expression of gender and other biases by confronting such views and behaviors. This can mean, for example, individual board members calling into question the assumptions of the consultant who asks, "Are you ready for a woman in this district?" In the reverse direction, it can mean the headhunter questioning board members' prejudicial foregone conclusions about the sex or marital status of the potential new hire.

The approaches to intervention around such biases vary considerably, along a continuum from least to most confrontational. The range includes using humor, applying nonjudgmental educative strategies to increase awareness of biases, modeling intolerance for demeaning or stereotypical comments, intervening when even minor transgressions occur in the process of interviewing candidates, or repudiating biasing remarks out of hand (Van Nostrand, 1993).

An illustration of how attempts at humor are used with the intent of building awareness is proffered by a headhunter who relates: "Sometimes, I've had to make people pay attention. I distinctly remember telling one board member who repeatedly used sexist language, 'You know, Harry, you're not recruiting a concubine, you're recruiting a superintendent.'" Another consultant tries to prevent a board from digressing to gender biases by asserting, "It doesn't matter whether they stand or sit when they go to the bathroom. It matters whether they can be a superintendent."

Although it's questionable how helpful to women the use of derogatory terms (concubine?) and bathroom humor are, the intent in both of these cases was to confront an expression of bias in the selection process. Again, each of these interventions involve taking a risk in what is often an intense and sensitive board-consultant working relationship.

School Board and Administrative Composition

The discussion thus far has centered on practices in which both headhunters and school boards engage to ensure gender and other diversities in superintendent searches. Also discovered in this study were several other practices that serve this same end and are exclusive to boards.

For example, some boards seek gender and racial/ethnic diversity in their own membership. According to several board members, this may be a necessary first step to modeling expectations for heterogeneous leadership of the educational system. Some African American candidates in this study confirmed that board diversity can influence their decision whether or not to apply to a particular district.

For example, a woman reports, "I had to think very carefully about whether or not I wanted to be the superintendent in that district at that time. This is very important: The makeup of the board was three African Americans and four Caucasians. One Caucasian female and three males, and two African American women and one African American male. So it was both male and Caucasian dominated." The double bind (Doughty, 1980; Ortiz & Ortiz, 1995) that racial/ethnic minority, female candidates face is evident in this qualified candidate's thinking. She hypothesized that her application would be viewed more favorably had either women or African Americans been in the majority on that board.

Previous research supports this candidate's hypothesis; that is, there is evidence that the racial and gender balance of school board membership is related to the race and gender of who gets hired as superintendent. Jackson and Cibulka's (1992) studies found that "cities with racially representative school boards are more likely to have an African-American superintendent than those which do not have representative boards" (p. 75). They defined representativeness as "having an African-American majority on the board or achieving an African-American membership which is within 10 percentage points of the percent of African-American students" (p. 75).

Marietti and Stout's (1994) research on 114 school boards in 19 different states found that higher proportions of female-majority boards hired female superintendents than did male-majority boards. Similarly, Radich's (1992) study of access to the superintendency in Washington State found that there were slightly greater proportions of women school board members in districts where women were hired as superintendents. Marietti and Stout (1994) also found that, compared to boards that select males, boards that hire female superintendents have greater numbers of females in other administrative positions in their district.

Within-district leadership development. Besides seeking heterogeneity within their own membership, some boards in this study try to foster increased diversity within their district's administration by overseeing formal structuring of opportunities for "growing their own" leaders. This typically appears in larger and urban school systems, where there is more likely to be a racially and ethnically diverse teaching cadre to build upon (Banks, 1995). It can take the form of creating teacher leadership and administrative internship opportunities within the school district, coupled with the more informal encouragement and recruitment of historically underrepresented group members discussed previously, so as to take advantage of those in-house opportunity structures for advancement.

For example, one board's districtwide leadership development structures include (a) encouraging principals to nominate teachers and novice administrators for its superintendent's special research and problem-solving team, (b) providing teacher-on-special-assignment roles wherein teachers may retain their tenure status while experimenting with broader leadership responsibilities, (c) making administrative internships available at many of its buildings, (d) collaborating with local university-based preparation programs to fill those internships with quality students of both genders and multiple cultures, and (e) promoting from within the district for more advanced leadership roles.

School Board Checks and Balances

These two illustrations (board member diversity and the district's opportunity structures) are examples of how attention to systemic issues can provide a more hospitable context for welcoming diversity in headhunting for superintendents. Beyond these broad connections, however, are board practices specific to search and selection for the superintendency.

For example, some board members explicitly inquire into headhunters' past record regarding diversity in finding and bringing to boards women and people of color in the searches they have assisted. These questions are raised at the inception of the process, when the board is entertaining search proposals from a number of different consultants. Such inquiries signal the board's interests or values somewhat circuitously.

Other board members address this issue more directly, articulating their expectations explicitly and insisting on seeing a slate of interviewees that includes women and/or minority group members. A board member recounts, "We had three very strong women on the board and simply said to our consultant, 'We want some female candidates.' It wasn't that we were dead set on hiring a female superintendent, but we certainly wanted to see some female candidates. We were very clear on that."

An African American board member from a different district is even more direct: "We did tell [our consultant] to recruit. Make sure the pool includes some women and minorities. As a school board member, I shouldn't have to tell you where to go find them, and I shouldn't have to bring them to you. But it needs to happen." Another board member explains, "I take a lot of ribbing on the board because I'm always the one to bring up gender. And I did that in our superintendent search as well. Well, gee, wouldn't it be nice to have a woman in that position? Not because a woman would be better qualified than any man. But because these are the kinds of role models we need to have for children, to see men and women in positions of authority."

Another way that boards work to ensure diversity in the process is to implement checks on the evaluative perspectives of their consultant. For example, individual board members may choose to participate more actively in the preliminary paper screening of applicants. Alternatively, some conduct independent reference checks of candidates both forwarded to them and eliminated by the head-hunter. These checks may include consulting with people outside of the conventional, predominantly white male networks relied upon by consultants. Some board members refer to this as a checks-and-balances approach, sometimes much like the stance they take on other actions that are recommended to them by their incumbent superintendent and within-district administrative leadership.

Other school board members explain such checks more as a function of their role expectations for the outside consultant. As one board member explains, "We saw the search consultant's role as technical assistance to us, rather than a strong screening function. We expected to do the screening ourselves." Although such a perspective may characterize a board's general approach to its operations, in this study, the references were specific to the preferred outcome of gender or racial heterogeneity in the superintendent search process.

Residency

Some boards also open up the search process to diversity by eliminating, or remaining flexible about, within-district residency requirements for the new superintendent hire. A consultant summarizes it this way: "When you make residency a requirement, you add on another limiting factor to your pool. It shrinks the pool before you even get to see any candidates, because some administrators just simply won't apply under those conditions." Another headhunter hypothesizes that residency requirements can disadvantage women candidates more so than men, given enduring societal norms that families tend to move their homes to follow the male, not the female, parent's career interests: "Men have traditionally had society's permission to relocate for job reasons and to say to the family, 'We're going.' At least in the past, many women haven't enjoyed that kind of social approval."

From a policy perspective, although virtually all school boards prize and expect high visibility and active participation in the local community by their superintendents, there are ways to achieve that goal apart from the location of residence, such as through clear job descriptions, annual board-superintendent leadership goals, and superintendent performance assessments. These may be reasonable alternatives to strict residency rules, especially for boards interested in opening up the superintendent search and selection process to as large and diverse a range of candidates as possible.

Summary and Implications

This chapter has provided numerous illustrations of what consultants and school board members do to open up superintendent search and selection processes to a diverse and wide gamut of educational leaders. Examples ranged from the underlying assumptions, values, and beliefs that drive commitments to equity; to building heterogeneity throughout varied leadership pipelines of educators; to the creation of presuperintendency opportunity structures for members of historically underrepresented groups to acquire additional leadership skills; to targeted recruitment of females and people of color; to specific modifications in common selection procedures.

All of these practices are geared to mitigating the gender and ethnic/racial biases that can limit access to the superintendency. They help to remove barriers and widen, rather than narrow, the pathways to this important educational leadership role. They also illustrate how attending to systemic issues can provide a more hospitable context for welcoming diversity in headhunting for superintendents.

What can you, as a potential future applicant, learn from these promising practices? First, it's clear that some consultants and boards have more of an interest in promoting diversity than others. You can find this out by using your own networks of contacts to inquire about reputations and records of placement. You can observe the demographic makeup of districts' and search firms' screening and interviewing teams to try to discern some clues about equity values. And you can study particular districts' practices of growing their own leaders: Are there systems in place for identifying and developing a diverse range of talent internally?

In addition to information-gathering, it's also important for you to be aware of reasons apart from competency that will contribute to your becoming part of a slate of semifinalists for some superintendencies. There may be times when you find yourself the only nonincumbent superintendent, or the only person of a particular color or sex among the candidates who progress through the various selection gates.

In some cases, your inclusion at this stage will be due to shallow concerns for appearances of political correctness. But as this chapter has shown, your inclusion also can be the result of genuine interest in creating opportunities for candidates who have traveled unconventional pathways in their careers; commitment to making educational leadership more closely reflect the gender and racial/ethnic backgrounds of student populations; or a valuing of the different perspectives and unique contributions that nontraditional leaders may bring to the superintendency.

You will probably have a better sense of which of these possible scenarios applies after your interviews. But because you will not know for sure, you should certainly approach all of your encounters assuming the most respectable of intentions on the parts of the consultant, selection committee, and board. If you don't or can't believe that, it will likely show, in which case it's probably better for you not to participate in the interview.

7

How Can You Get the Most From the Network?

Mary Hannick is in her second superintendency. She acquired her first in 1978, a time when there was just one other female superintendent in her state. Mary's typically direct when she speaks. She summarizes her views on accessing the superintendency like this: "I think it's a very subtle obstacle course put up. There's a mystique about how to get a superintendency. There really is. That you have to know all the right people and have all the skills already in place. Well, you don't need to know everyone or everything. That's the mystique. That's what the current superintendents don't tell others coming up. Or, I think, more to the point, they let some people in on these big secrets but not others."

Anne Hermann disagrees, at least in part. Anne signed her first superintendency contract 3 months ago. She agrees that you certainly don't need to "have all the skills already in place" to obtain a superintendency. But she views as essential "knowing the right people." As she puts it, "Developing and maintaining connections within the network is as important as acquiring the skills to do the job. For me, it helped to do my job well and have a good reputation. But I also worked as hard to stay in touch with people who could put a good word in for me here and there, and who could get me information when I needed it."

As Anne and Mary's perspectives suggest, a combination of competencies and connections are important to accessing the superintendency. How can you get the most from the various administrators, search consultants, university professors, school board members, and others key to obtaining this educational leadership role?

129

This study's participants found numerous ways to connect with and influence these informal networks. You can, too. Here's how.

Create Opportunities for Skill Development

One way is to continue to expand your leadership skills. Cuban's (1988) and Johnson's (1996) research underscores the importance of the educational, managerial, and political competencies of school superintendents. You can be proactive about structuring opportunities to enable yourself to acquire, practice, and refine skills in each of these three areas.

For example, at the least experienced end of the continuum, this study's candidates recounted instances in which they took the initiative to write grants to generate funds needed to support their own internships for preliminary administrative licensure. Many worked closely with university faculty to secure the most rigorous and challenging kinds of internships available.

After gaining initial leadership experiences locally, some traveled considerable distances to assume educational leadership roles that they felt would fill in gaps in their skills base. Others asked superordinates for (and were given) additional responsibilities in leadership areas not under their normal purview in order to gain experiences that their existing jobs did not afford them.

Some volunteered to chair committees or take the lead on initiatives they knew would increase their own competencies and visibility in the region or state. A candidate's account summarizes this well: "I studied and dissected what the superintendency is. Then I went and got myself as many of those kinds of experiences as I could, regardless of the job title. As an elementary principal, I asked my superintendent if I could be involved in negotiations. As a curriculum coordinator, I asked to be involved in the districtwide budget process. I volunteered for anything and everything, so I could go down that checklist of all the things that make up the superintendent's job, to create a portfolio for myself."

Gleaning the most you can from these portfolios or repertoires of experiences, however, is also key. One way of ensuring that is to approach difficult job assignments as problems to be solved rather than tasks to be accomplished. On one hand, a problem-solving perspective can help you refine your analytical skills in identifying component obstacles and dynamics in complex situations. It can also help you develop the habit of generating three or four different solutions to problems. This can provide valuable practice in approaching issues from alternative frames of reference (e.g., educational or technical, political, interpersonal), thus contributing to your skills base as a future superintendent.

Also, because working directly with the school board is a unique feature of the superintendency, it's essential to acquire experiences in that arena. Some candidates in this study sought opportunities to serve as the primary contact with the board on particular district initiatives. Of course, maintaining clear communication with the incumbent superintendent is critical to such initiatives, as is debriefing with him or her as a "critical friend," to learn the most you can from your direct contacts with the board.

Ask for feedback. Post hoc debriefings of your relationship-building with school boards are just one vehicle for getting a different perspective on your work. However, to help develop your leadership skills for the superintendency, you should be proactive about soliciting feedback on your performance *throughout* your administrative career.

In this study, even when feedback was not forthcoming or was only cursorily attended to in formal performance reviews, savvy candidates requested additional assessment about their strengths and weaknesses from superordinates and respected others. Some sought counsel about ways to improve and about ways to handle particular situations differently the next time. If they interviewed for positions and were not offered the job, many attempted to obtain specifics about the reasons why, with the goal of addressing whatever deficiencies might be identified.

If asked, the headhunters who observe board interviews of candidates will sometimes provide information about what, in their opinion, appeared to click or not click with the interviewers. The candidates who participated in this study underscore the usefulness of these practices: "It was helpful when [headhunter] sat down with me [after not advancing to finalist] and said, 'You really have to do these things in the next interview.' I needed that. I needed someone to say to me, 'This is what boards are looking for. This is how you can present what you've done.'"

Long before the interview stage, you can also solicit feedback on the written materials you may be considering submitting with your applications. In this study, some candidates shared their resumés with headhunters and selected university faculty, seeking their assessment and advice for ways to improve their presentation of self. A consultant confirms how this looks from his perspective: "[Candidate] heard me speak at a conference for aspiring superintendents. At those events, I always say, 'If you want to come and talk to me at any time, you're welcome.' And she has done that. She's called me. She's asked for help with her resumé. She met with me and asked me to review things. *Those* are the people who are going to get ahead."

Participate in formal professional development. Incumbent administrators; professional organizations (of teachers, administrators, and school boards); and university-based administrator preparation programs sometimes also provide either structured workshops or one-to-one counseling for specific job-getting skills and career development. Participate in as many of these as you can.

These opportunities often center on awareness- and competency-building in interviewing for the superintendency, but they may also include understanding search and selection processes, developing effective superintendent-school board relationships, designing and executing entry plans for new leadership roles, improving one's resumé and credentials, and understanding educational law, to name just a few relevant issues.

With respect to interview preparation, an incumbent woman superintendent recalls, "Before I came out here for my board interviews, I attended a role-playing simulation that was offered by the state women administrators' group. That got me thinking about, 'These are the kinds of things you'll probably be asked. Here's an approach to the interview you might want to take. Let's think about the kinds of answers you're going to give. Let's practice articulating them so it's clear you know what you're talking about. Because you do.'"

Find and Make Mentors

Many candidates in this study sought and used multiple mentors. There are numerous lessons to be learned from this. Rather than relying exclusively on the relationship-building and career sponsorship that may occur naturally between you and some colleagues or superordinates, it is usually wise to seek and find mentors from others outside your immediate circle for specific purposes, such as assisting in the development of particular communications skills or, perhaps, gaining greater familiarity with financial procedures.

In this study, some candidates not only sought such assistance but expected and gently demanded it, particularly of administrators known to be key sources of referrals for superintendency vacancies. Most were persistent. Some were, to an extent, self-promoting. All were careful to avoid arrogance or immodesty.

Career mentors may be incumbent school administrators of varied titles, members and leaders of superintendent and other educational professional organizations, or university professors. Each can serve different purposes for you. Some can help simply in terms of personal encouragement, confidence-building, and inspiration to pursue ever more challenging leadership roles. Some will be key to creating, and inviting you to participate in, opportunities to increase skills and understandings. Some will have particular areas of expertise that they can share with you.

At other times, you will want to be able to call upon mentors who have access to information very specific to the individual districts to which you may be considering applying. What's the board really like behind the scenes? How have collective bargaining relationships been with teachers and other unionized staff? What has been the history of superintendent turnover in that district?

You may request that this kind of insider information be translated into specific advice about for which districts' superintendency openings to apply and which openings spell trouble from the start and should be avoided. These perspectives can become quite useful to you when preparing for board and community interviews because they will help you to better understand the context within which questions are asked.

For example, a candidate in this study vividly recalls, "I'd call [my university mentor] and say, 'East Cupcake school district has got an opening. What do you think?' He might be enthusiastic or he might say, 'Well, I don't know if you want to go there.' It might be that they had a reputation for being too fiscally conservative. Or that they had an element on the board that was divisive. Or that they beat up on other superintendents. Stuff like that. He would share that kind of information with me."

Similarly, a consultant explains, "I do a lot of talking with candidates and possible applicants. And I'm very candid about the district. I'll tell them about the fights that are going on. There's a faction here, or we've got a high school principal who is very weak.

Whatever the reality is. No sugar coating. This is what you'd be going into. Here are the potentials." In this way, these influentials serve as a resource for all potential applicants, and they could be mentors for you.

Nurture All Connections

Although virtually all experienced teachers and administrators have some professional networks, women and people of color may not have access to as extensive a network of influentials as white males do (Wheatley, 1981). For example, sensitive inside information may be more readily accessible through informal, same-sex inter-actions on the golf course, or over a drink at a conference—two activi-ties which are likely to go unquestioned when the participants are all male, but could be cause for notice when women so engage. It's im-portant to be aware that your own opportunities for mentor making may be constrained in some ways by these kinds of sociocultural factors.

However, there is still much you can do and much that can be learned from others. For example, in this study, all who were suc-cessful in obtaining one or more superintendencies attended to and developed multiple connections throughout regional, statewide, and national networks of experienced administrators and search consultants. As this candidate attests, connections that might not seem powerful at present can turn into key contacts in the future: "I felt I had to get to know people and not be quick to write anyone off. People I might have not worked well with initially were able to help me later in my career. So I spent, and continue to spend, a significant time in keeping contacts. It's often difficult, but I never got so in-volved in my work that I couldn't join organizations and meet people for lunch or dinner."

Other candidates ensured that their names and faces were "out there" by making contributions not only within their own districts, but also in their regions and professional organizations. A candidate explains, "We have to be known in the network, and one way of get-ting known is to do something for others outside your school system. The reality is that, eventually, somebody is going to make a phone call to one of them about you. So, the more people that you know, the more people who have firsthand experience with your work, the better chances you have of getting that next job. I absolutely believe that and have built a successful career on it."

Apply for the Superintendency

The kind of individual agency and proactivity that has been central to this chapter focuses on your accessing and cultivating professional networks of contacts, mentors, and sponsors. Perhaps it goes without saying, but another important step is to *apply* for superintendencies, whether or not you are recruited or encouraged to do so.

In this study, many candidates were being selective, and most were doing a great deal of homework about the districts to which they were considering submitting their applications. Some employed networks to keep informed of possible and future openings, rather than waiting for vacancy advertisements to be posted. Others used data available on the World Wide Web for information about superintendent vacancies (e.g., some state school board associations allow applications to be filed electronically for the searches on which they consult). Many state education departments also provide extensive Web-accessible information on individual school districts. These can be useful sources of data on budgets, other financial records, aggregated student test performance, and so on. Again, coupled with the information available from personal networks, these sorts of data on districts can be key to your decision to apply for a particular superintendency or not.

Summary and Implications

This study found that members of historically underrepresented groups are being proactive about their own advancement in the existing systems of access to the school superintendency. They find ways to accumulate the educational, managerial, and political skills needed to make themselves viable candidates for the position. They create opportunities for themselves to acquire new administrative experiences. They solicit feedback on their performance so as to hone and expand existing strengths. They give serious attention to their growth as educational leaders, and they participate in professional development. They find mentors for different purposes and draw on others' expertise and connections. They nurture relationships—even ones that don't appear immediately beneficial but may prove powerful in the future.

On one level, these are examples you may emulate; illustrations from which anyone interested in pursuing a superintendency can learn. On another level, these purposeful activities demonstrate how nonmajority people develop strategies for negotiating the complexities of a profession predominated by white males for more than a century. Whereas several previous chapters centered on systemic and cultural features that can work against access to the superintendency by women and people of color, this chapter illustrates how inroads can be made. Accordingly, this research supports Edson's (1995) findings and Grogan's (1996) conclusions that it is encouraging that women and minorities are finding "ways around some of the structures that were potentially inhibiting" and are "resisting discouragement thus far, by holding on to their aspirations in the face of difficulties" (Grogan, 1996, p. 5).

Prior research underscores the salience of informal systems of sponsorship for the career mobility of those different from historic incumbents in leadership positions (Banks, 1995; Hennig & Jardim, 1977; Hudson, 1994; Miklos, 1988; Ortiz & Marshall, 1988). Bell and Chase's (1996) studies found that women in the superintendency recognize that "having the support of male colleagues and connections to powerful men is necessary to the development of their careers" (p. 124). Like Bell and Chase, this chapter confirms that "to be well connected to white men is to be integrated into the power structure and support networks of the occupation" (Bell & Chase, 1996, p. 129).

As Biklen, Bogad, and Luschen (1996) suggest, it's important to avoid portraying females or people of color as either victims or members of unified, oppressed groups. Instead, they are complex, active agents who experience many messy and contradictory expectations. For women in the superintendency, Chase (1995) calls this messiness "ambiguous empowerment"; that is, the "contradictory experiences of power and subjection" (p. xi).

The initiatives described in this chapter also illustrate how aspirants to the superintendency successfully deal with what Bell's (1995) research found to be the contrary statuses of outsider and insider, belonging and not belonging, for those who do not look like the majority of incumbent superintendents. You, too, may benefit from these strategies in your own career.

8

Conclusions: So What?

Other books aimed at current and prospective school administrators often focus on individual responsibility for aspirations, career choices, and success in overcoming obstacles along the challenging pathways to top educational leadership roles (e.g., Black & English, 1996; Carter et al., 1993; Pigford & Tonnsen, 1993). They are rich sources of advice about appropriate preparation, the accumulation of relevant experiences, and strategies for shaping oneself to the job.

In contrast, this volume balances attention to the individual, institutional, and cultural dynamics involved in how experienced administrators obtain superintendencies. Three major themes underlie these dynamics.

First, there are systemic regularities to superintendent search and selection processes that, although often invisible to the public, can be brought to light and demystified. Despite minor variations by state, district, or consultant, there is a remarkable sameness to school boards' and selection committees' modus operandi. As described in Chapters 1 through 3, these include institutionalized practices related to initial preparations for the search, advertisement and recruitment for the position, preliminary screening of applicants, narrowing of the field of candidates, interviews of semifinalists, and final selection and hiring. Key behind-the-scenes influences center on consultants' and veteran superintendents' telephone recruiting, confidential reference checking, school board executive sessions, and private interviews with candidates.

A second major theme is that a number of sociocultural biases and other unwritten rules of superintendent search and selection present unique challenges for women and others who are unlike most incumbent, white male superintendents. These were the foci of

137

Chapters 4 and 5. The unwritten rules include tacit understandings about desired qualifications, how "best" is defined, experiential background, age, marital status, and single parenthood, as well as the subtle devaluing of career paths more frequently traveled by females and people of color in education. Cultural biases relate to prevalent belief systems associated with merit, gender, and race, as well as overt discrimination.

The third theme of this volume is that understanding the stated and unstated selection rules can lead to successfully accessing the superintendency. These understandings are significant for all those engaged in this employment pursuit. However, insider information is particularly important for those historically marginalized from the most influential networks (e.g., females) and those who may not share the same cultural background as majority incumbents (e.g., people of color). Implications for prospective candidates of both genders and all colors were discussed in each chapter. Some implications relate to the nitty-gritty of common school board and consultant practices; others to the broader systemic and cultural dynamics at work.

Differing Perspectives

Interestingly, males and females—and minorities and nonminorities—disagree on questions of whether, how, or to whatdegree gender and racial/ethnic biases affect women and people of color. This is true in educational administration, other fields, and society at large.

More specifically, research in education and business demonstrates wide gaps in perceptions of barriers and discrimination in employment by both sex and race/ethnicity. For example, in a study of top executives in Fortune 1000 companies, females ranked "male stereotyping and preconceptions of women" and "exclusion from informal networks" as the top two obstacles to women's advancement in corporate leadership (Catalyst, 1996). In contrast, male CEOs ranked "lack of significant general management or line experience" and "insufficient time in the pipeline" as the top two barriers. Relatedly, whereas a third of female executives believe "an inhospitable corporate culture" holds women back, male CEOs are much less likely to attribute women's underrepresentation in the highest ranks of management to such cultural or systemic factors (Maruca, 1997).

In education, previous large-scale national surveys indicate that 84% of female superintendents and 73% of racial/ethnic minority superintendents view discriminatory hiring practices against women as a "major" or "minor problem," whereas 53% of male superintendents see it as "little" or "no problem" (Glass, 1992, p. 62). Similarly, higher percentages of women and minority superintendents than male superintendents see discriminatory hiring practices against minorities as a major/minor problem; higher proportions of male superintendents than women or minority superintendents see it as little/no problem (Glass, 1992, p. 62).

With respect to the general public, a 1997 national opinion poll conducted by the Joint Center for Political and Economic Studies demonstrates that people of color and whites have very different perceptions about racism in American society (Gleaves-Hirsch, 1997). Whereas whites acknowledge that some discrimination against African Americans exists, Blacks see discrimination against them as common (Gleaves-Hirsch, 1997).

Also relevant to the perceptions of the general public is the widespread unfriendliness toward affirmative action that is characteristic of the 1990s. This unfriendliness is often tied to beliefs that females and minorities are accorded unfair advantages in American society, and that reverse discrimination against white men is prevalent (Dovidio et al., 1997). Yet most economic and social indicators belie the latter; that is, Caucasian males continue to earn more money and occupy higher proportions of leadership positions than do females or people of color, whether in government, religious institutions, education, medicine, law, or private business.

Who's Got It Right?

It's clear that the historically disenfranchised see things differently from the historically privileged. It's also clear that, until relatively recently, little attention has been given to the perspectives of females and people of color in educational leadership research (Banks, 1995; Schmuck & Dunlap, 1995; Shakeshaft, 1989, 1995). In all likelihood, each of these disparate viewpoints sheds some light on "the truth."

Accordingly, this volume has brought multiple perspectives to bear on the issue of superintendent search and selection in order to contribute to a more complete understanding of practice. This study captures the perspectives of males and females, Caucasians and African Americans, school board members and search consultants, and successful and unsuccessful applicants for superintendencies.

Other research drawn upon in this volume includes varied combinations of administrator, superintendent, school board member, and headhunter sources. For example, Glass (1992) surveyed a national sample of incumbent superintendents. Chase and Bell's (1990, 1994) research included superintendents, school board members, consultants, state-level officials, and community members. Rose's (1969) study of superintendent sponsors and sponsorees spanned eight regions, including northeastern, eastern, central, southern, western, and northwestern United States. Tieman (1968) surveyed consultants and school boards involved in the recruitment and selection of superintendents in Ohio and Illinois. Martin (1978) studied Illinois school board presidents' perspectives. Magowan's (1979) research used a panel of experts drawn from all parts of the country to identify the top five nationally recognized consultants included in her study. Rickabaugh's (1986) sources were headhunters in Wisconsin, Michigan, Iowa, Minnesota, and Illinois. Swart (1990) studied consultants, superintendents, and board presidents in New York. Radich's (1992) research included superintendents, school board members, and consultants in the state of Washington. Kamler (1995) studied headhunters in New York. Roberts (1996) included consultants in Massachusetts, New Hampshire, New York, Pennsylvania, Vermont, and Virginia.

Thus, this volume brings together the most comprehensive range of research to date on the topic of superintendent search and selection. Moreover, few others have considered issues of gender or color in their analyses of school board and consultant practices (the exceptions are Chase and Bell, 1990, 1994; Kamler, 1995; Magowan, 1979; Ortiz, 1998; and Radich, 1992). Published information on these issues, in an accessible format, is long overdue, as is balanced attention to both implications for individuals and prospects for improving the system through more open access to the superintendency.

Change the System

How can current and future educational leaders play a part in changing institutional norms and practices that can limit diversity in the superintendency? Several strategies center on creating awareness of imbalances and establishing a culture hospitable to the leadership and advancement of women and people of color in both superintendent and nonsuperintendent administrative roles. That means doing some preliminary homework.

First, you can examine existing information on administrative employment patterns in your district and region. This will provide important baseline data against which future change may be compared. Information can be collected about the numbers of males, females, and people of color in leadership; the nature and titles of the positions they hold; histories of promotions, as well as cutbacks in administration; and salaries. For example, who stays and remains successful? Who is let go when downsizing occurs? What about balance among staff and line positions, and among elementary and secondary schools? Patterns should be analyzed in terms of gender and race/ethnicity. The results of analyses can be shared with the school board and other district personnel who influence the hiring and advancement of school administrators.

Second, and dependent upon what baseline figures reveal, you can set targets and time lines for improving the diversity among the district or region's leadership. This is a matter of setting clear goals, just as you do with other institutional priorities. Your baseline data and trends analysis will enable you to monitor and assess progress accurately over time, rather than relying on murky recollections or general impressions of how diverse the administrative team has been. Again, keep appropriate constituencies informed and involved by sharing your data and goals.

Structure Opportunities

A third strategy involves creating systems for grooming high-potential leadership talent, with diversity outcomes structured into the process. Some organizations are doing this through a combination of strategic mentoring and succession planning. What does that look like? Basically, three steps are involved. Applied to educational settings, it means, first, having all current administrators identify three individuals with the potential to succeed them in their position: (a) one person who could step into the job, on an emergency basis, virtually immediately; (b) a second who could grow into the position in 3 to 5 years; and (c) a third individual who is a woman or person of color.

After identifying these three people, it then becomes critical to provide encouragement and support by creating opportunities for them to expand their skills and gain additional administrative experience. This is an important step because we know that experiencing success with leadership responsibilities can inspire greater interest in administration—even if the person is initially reluctant or undecided about pursuing a formal educational leadership role (Edson, 1995). Be aware, however, that providing females and people of color with "stretch" experiences may mean putting them in charge of departments or schools that have never before reported to a woman or minority. Accordingly, the seemingly straightforward structuring of developmental opportunities for those marginalized in the past can involve profound cultural change. The achievement of a critical mass of nontraditional leaders in diverse roles will help ameliorate initial culture shock for both the individual and the institution.

The third step in this strategic mentoring and succession planning system is to assist each of the three identified individuals in making connections to other school leaders and administrators. As this volume has shown, those informal networks and communications channels are important to professional advancement. They are also important to on-the-job success. Organizations committed to diversifying their leadership must support on-the-job success and retention, as well as equitable access, to sustain strong administrative teams (Tallerico et al., 1993). Especially in the case of historically underrepresented group members, the loss of even a few can significantly affect diversity goals.

Use statewide and regional structures. In many instances, individual school systems can take advantage of other organizations similarly interested in structuring opportunities to expand the pool of qualified candidates for the superintendency. For example, statewide and regional career development conferences are sometimes aimed at educating actively aspiring superintendents and potential superintendents about the realities of obtaining and succeeding in the superintendency. Usually, these conferences are attended by experienced administrators, with invitations for nominations channeled through sitting superintendents.

For this study, I attended several such conferences as an observer and was able to conduct informal interviews with a dozen nominees. As it turns out, some aspirants learned of these opportunities serendipitously from outside their own districts, presented themselves to their superintendent, and asked to be nominated. Others were approached personally by the superintendent, shown the call for nominations, and asked, "Is this something you'd be interested in?"

In contrast to these two forms of nomination, what appeared to be most motivating to the nominees was when the superintendent not only personalized the invitation but accompanied it with positive comments about his or her esteem for both the nominee's abilities and the value of this kind of preparation. To wit, "I think you could do this job and would be very good at it. I'd like to select you to attend this upcoming conference to learn more about how to prepare for the role."

What these different approaches illustrate is how the power of institutional sponsorship may be increased by being sensitive to the manner in which the nomination is made. Some candidates sensed a half-heartedness to the invitation, some saw it as a neutral experience, and some found it enthusiastic and validating.

Attend to Feeder Pools

As some school boards and consultants in this study revealed, a long-term perspective on leadership development can ultimately reap rewards in terms of greater diversity in applicant pools for the superintendency (see Chapter 6). Another way to increase the number of women and people of color in leadership pipelines is to provide institutional support for administrative internships. That means money, time, and human resources for appropriate coaching and mentoring.

We know that there are lots of females and some people of color participating in university-based administrator preparation programs. Without access to full-time, paid internships, the best and brightest from those programs cannot gain the kinds of meaningful, entry-level experiences that will enable them to become the next generation of school superintendents. In the long-term pipeline to the superintendency, a dysfunctional and unnecessary bottleneck occurs without strong internships. The creation and funding of such opportunities—again, accompanied by diversity goals—is a concrete action that can be taken on an institutional level.

It's not uncommon for boards and administrators to lament the small numbers of applicants in recent searches for high school principals and superintendents (Barker, 1997; Houston, 1998; McAdams, 1998). If you are in a position to raise a question about this, ask, "How has our organization contributed to, or constrained, the growth of the pool of potential leaders by the availability of entry-level internships in our district, region, or state?" And, "Of the interns we have supported in the past, what has the gender and racial/ethnic balance been?" By raising questions such as these, you may influence local community belief systems and draw attention to institutional responsibilities for promoting leadership and equity.

Screen Applicants Equitably

It is likely that you currently are, or soon will be, in a position to influence decision making in your district about the selection and hiring of educational administrators. Who gets recruited into, or screened out of, applicant pools is a key institutional responsibility. As the research in this volume has demonstrated, these are also the functions most susceptible to cultural biases and myths about the paths traveled, and the potential for leadership, of those who look different from the majority of people who have led the public schools in the past.

What else can be done, both at the paper screening and interview stage, to promote equity in the superintendency and other administrative positions? Here are seven ideas:

1. Balance screening and interview committee membership by sex and race/ethnicity wherever possible. Include advocates for diversity on selection teams. Moody's (1983) research, for example, found that Black candidates' chances for advancement were increased when selection committees were chaired by Blacks.

2. Advance applicants with evidence of educational accomplishments and leadership potential, broadly defined. Historically, narrow definitions of "career path" may have excluded talented individuals needlessly (see Chapter 5). For example, there is no evidence that a person who has served as a high school principal will make a better superintendent than a person who has been an elementary principal. Similarly, there are many outstanding principals who have never served as assistant principals. Do not confuse previous educational position titles with leadership accomplishments and ideas. The latter are what's important.

3. Focus on competencies and skills, wherever they were acquired, rather than lifestyle, family, home location, or issues irrelevant to job performance. As you know, inquiries about marital status, age, number of children, and sexual orientation are all illegal. Also, expectations or policies requiring within-district residency can unnecessarily limit the pool of prospective applicants.

4. View curricular and instructional expertise as strengths, not liabilities, for school management and leadership positions, again, regardless of the grade levels at which the expertise was acquired. Many experienced women and administrators of color can be found in staff, rather than line, positions, and elementary, rather than secondary, settings, leading important educational programs.

5. Obtain references from members of women's and minority educators' professional organizations. As this research has shown, the perspectives of white males typically dominate background checks, nominations of candidates, and screening recommendations. Diversifying here may provide new insights and opportunities.

6. Intervene to halt any discussion related to physical appearance. For example, there is no evidence that the best disciplinarians are tall, the strongest leaders large-framed, or the smartest administrators Caucasian. These are biases and myths that limit both the pipeline and access to the superintendency.

7. Ask the same interview questions of all candidates. Use standardized rating forms that focus interviewers on competen-

cies and accomplishments rather than job titles. Educate interviewers about the subtle biases that can distract raters from important selection criteria.

Improve Induction Systems

Another promising systemic approach to fostering and maintaining diversity in the superintendency centers on providing supportive programming for first- and second-year superintendents. In this study, there was evidence that varied combinations of statewide superintendents' organizations, regional superintendents, and university outreach providers are collaborating to design and deliver specialized professional development opportunities for this unique audience.

These collaboratives can take many forms. In some less structured models, telephone lists of volunteer superintendents and their unique areas of expertise are shared with novices, along with encouragement to call upon those resources whenever needed. In more structured models, veteran superintendents in a region may be paired with novices for ongoing communication and personalized kinds of coaching. A consultant describes a multicounty model that was developed by two collaborating regional superintendents and is led by a retired superintendent: "Together, we have over 50 districts in our supervisory areas. Each year, about 14 or 15 of those districts have new superintendents. Many are first-timers. So, we've created a program where we have applied for a special grant and used those funds to hire an ex-superintendent to work with each of these individuals. He takes them through board meetings and agenda development, community development, how to pass a budget. It's all heavy-duty, hands-on stuff. Sometimes, he coaches them before meetings, watches meetings, gives them a hotline to call. It provides a safe place for a rookie to say, 'I don't have a clue.' They hesitate to admit that to me. They can't tell their board they don't have a clue. This provides new superintendents a safe place to grow."

Because women and people of color are likely to be among the newest appointees to these positions, these kinds of supportive induction practices can serve to promote and maintain diversity in the superintendency. Some researchers have found that the achievement of a "critical mass," rather than isolated token participation, of women and other historically marginalized group members is key to both the sustenance of diverse leadership in organizations and the provision of diverse role models for others to follow (Kanter, 1977). The latter provides the link to the current and prospective candidates for the superintendency who are a central focus of this book.

Shape Belief Systems

Changing the discourse about prospective applicants to the superintendency is another way to affect the overall context of employment for this important leadership role. What does that mean? It means changing prevalent talk in the professional community—talk that is largely negative and sometimes ill-informed. It means acknowledging and emphasizing the strengths of current pools of candidates, thereby countering the more commonly held perception that the pool is weak.

As a headhunter in this study describes recent scuttlebutt: "I hear a lot from other consultants who have been superintendents that 'The pool was stronger when I was a candidate; I had to fight my way to the top. But they just aren't there today.' Well, I don't find that. We need to change the negative perception that's out there. I find there are many good candidates available."

Yes, a limited amount of research has shown that the number of applicants per superintendent search today is not as great as it was in prior years (O'Connell, 1995). But there is no solid evidence that the pool is of lesser quality. One reason that the pool looks different today is that there are more women in it than there were 20 years ago. You can help shape community and professional belief systems that influence access to the superintendency by underscoring that it's a different and smaller pool, not necessarily an inadequate or inferior one.

The size of the apparent current pool may be a function of lack of systematic outreach to administrators who look different from those who have predominated in the superintendency in the past. Another consultant in this study reports, "I am concerned that the pool seems sparse to some people. I don't think it is, and I've conducted many successful searches over the past 7 years. I think not everyone is doing enough to attract a broader range of candidates. If everyone did, the pool would seem great to more people."

Why Bother?

In sum, there are numerous ways that institutions and individuals can take responsibility for improving the access of women and people of color to every level of administrative leadership, including the school superintendency. Taken together, the strategies suggested in this chapter revolve around (a) eliminating outdated biases about who gets to be a leader, where, when, and under what circumstances; (b) questioning professional practices that do not serve equity and diversity values; (c) shaping community belief systems; and (d) creating opportunities that nurture the aspirations and achievements of a strong, diverse pool of administrative applicants.

It is also evident that many of the strategies suggested here require additional or redirected effort. For this reason, I close this volume with several reminders of why the effort is warranted.

First, education deserves the benefit of the diverse perspectives and experiences that different kinds of educators can bring to school administration. Put simply, it's the smart thing to do.

Second, we are currently underutilizing the diversity of talent and potential among our teaching ranks. Thus, it's the practical thing to do.

Third, equal opportunity in employment is guaranteed by Title VII of the 1964 Civil Rights Act and the 1963 Equal Pay Act (Bank, 1997). It's the legal thing to do.

Fourth, all children, no matter where they live, should see both genders and all colors in leadership roles in every occupation and institution, including education. It's the socially responsible thing to do.

Fifth, it is morally objectionable to ignore inequities in the attainments of men, women, and people of color. It's the right thing to do.

Importance of the position. Although equalizing access to all leadership positions is smart, practical, legally required, and socially responsible, nowhere is it more important to use every available pool of educational talent than in the superintendency. Numerous researchers have found that superintendents are key to the development, implementation, and maintenance of educational innovations in schools and districts (Bjork, 1993; Bredeson, 1996; Carter & Cunningham, 1997; Johnson, 1996; Leithwood, 1995). Robinson and Bickers (1990) contend that a school district's success depends, in large part, on the effectiveness of its superintendent. Holdaway and Genge (1995) demonstrate that superintendents' actions can have important, indirect effects on students' achievements. Hoyle's (1993) work with the American Association of School Administrators (AASA) Commission on Standards for the Superintendency recognizes that superintendents provide leadership and inspiration in school districts across the nation and that, to a great extent, the quality of America's schools depends on the leadership of superintendents. Ortiz (1991) and Norton et al. (1996) found that, through the position of superintendent, leaders have the authority and expertise to make a positive difference in the culture of the system and student learning.

In sum, the superintendency is an important educational leadership position for America's schools. Moreover, a change in leadership of a district can have a major impact on the school community (Johnson, 1996; Miklos, 1988). Consequently, the search for and selection of superintendents are among the most significant responsibilities of school boards (Brown, 1992; Chion-Kenney, 1994; Hord & Estes, 1993). Providing fair and open access to all potential sources of quality candidates is an important part of exercising this responsibility well.

Final Remarks

So here's to understanding and improving access to the superintendency. On one hand, this book demystifies search and selection, taking you behind the scenes to learn about a process largely invisible to the public. On the other hand, it offers prospects for change by identifying ways to be inclusive and fair in tapping diverse pools of talent.

You should now be better equipped to obtain a superintendency for yourself. And you should also have a repertoire of strategies for leading the kinds of systemic changes needed to increase equity and diversity in the recruitment and selection of educational administrators.

I leave you with three challenges: Change the unwritten rules that delegitimize certain backgrounds and pathways. Expose the biases that downplay institutional responsibility for improving leadership diversity. Share the access.

Appendix: Research Methods

This volume draws upon two principal sources of information. One source was a comprehensive review of research and other literatures relevant to the topics of (a) the superintendency, (b) search and selection practices, and (c) issues of gender and race/ethnicity in educational administration. Articles in scholarly and practitioner journals, books, and unpublished dissertations were included in this review. Emphasis was given to works written between 1965 and the present.

The other source of data was an in-depth case study of superintendent search and selection practices in one of the largest and most diverse states in the nation: New York. I conducted this original research over a 2-year period, 1996 to 1998. Qualitative methods of data collection were employed, including semistructured interviews, participant observation, and document analyses. Case study results were compared and contrasted to the findings that emerged from the literature review described above. Although both sets of findings are integrated within this volume, most of the direct quotes come from informants from the case study. The intent of this presentation style was to enliven previous research findings with the actual words of recent key participants in superintendent search and selection decision making.

Interviews for the Case Study

Who were these key informants? A total of 75 people were formally interviewed for the case study. A major strength of this investigation—and what distinguishes it from most previous research, with the exception of Chase and Bell (1990, 1994)—is that it draws upon the experiences and perspectives of school board members, search consultants, and recent applicants for superintendencies. These are the three groups most intimately connected with current superintendent search and selection. Hence, triangulation of data provided by these distinct sources allows an understanding of practice that would be impossible if any of the three were omitted.

More specifically, 25 school board members, 25 search consultants, and 25 recent candidates were interviewed. Interviews typically lasted about 2 hours, with a range of 1 to 4 hours. Most occurred in person, although some were conducted via telephone because of distance or other logistical considerations. All but two were audiotaped and transcribed verbatim for later analysis. Consistent with norms of qualitative research, interviewees were purposefully selected to provide as wide a range of perspectives as possible.

Headhunters. For example, I sought participation of each of the various "categories" of search consultants that exist, approximately paralleling the proportion of searches that that group facilitates in the state. That is, during the 2 years in which data were collected, national consultants conducted about 9% of New York superintendent searches; consultants who practice primarily locally conducted about 12% of searches; the state school board association conducted about 16% of searches; and regional superintendents conducted about 58% of all searches in the state. (The latter are known as BOCES, or Boards of Cooperative Educational Services superintendents; they are the rough equivalent of what would be county, intermediate unit, or regional service center superintendents in other states.) Accordingly, the case study sample of 25 search consultants included 2 national consultants, 7 who practice primarily locally, 2 who work for the state school board association, and 14 regional superintendents.

The state professional association of school superintendents maintains a listing of search consultants who operate within the state. That association also keeps records of superintendency vacancies throughout the state. I was able to analyze these records over a 2-year period to identify a pool of consultants from which to request interviews.

From that pool, I targeted interviewees who had assisted boards in different regions of the state and in districts of different sizes. I also purposely sought diversity by gender and race/ethnicity of consultants. This was a challenge, because only a handful of people of color serve as search consultants nationally, and males far outnumber females in all categories of consultants. As a result, 24 of the 25 consultants interviewed were Caucasian, and the other was African American; 6 were female, and 19 were male.

School board members. Only about 5% of this state's school boards typically conduct superintendent searches themselves; that is, without the assistance of a consultant. I specifically targeted boards that had conducted searches within the past 5 years. Within those boards, I purposely sought board members who had served long enough to have participated in at least two different superintendent searches. I did this for three reasons.

First, I wanted to draw upon insights that may have accrued from multiple experiences with search and selection processes. Second, multiple experiences would allow them to draw comparisons among different ways of conducting searches (e.g., by themselves, with the assistance of an outside facilitator, with different consultants at different times). Third, I wished to minimize participants' concerns that I might be seeking to expose particulars about their incumbent superintendent, rather than focusing on the study of practice in more general terms.

The state school board association and six regional associations of school boards within the state helped identify boards and board members who met these selection criteria. From that pool, I then purposely sought diversity by gender, race/ethnicity, and region of the state, as had been done for consultant selection. Of the 25 board members interviewed, 24 were Caucasian, and 1 was African American; 13 were male, and 12 were female.

Applicants. Consultants, school board members, and the state association of women school administrators assisted in identifying recent candidates for superintendent vacancies. From that pool, I selected 25 to interview, purposely seeking a range in terms of applying for a first or subsequent superintendency, being successful or unsuccessful in obtaining the position, race/ethnicity, and region of state where applied. Because males predominated in the other two categories of interviewees (consultants and school board members), I intentionally included more females than males in my selection, so that, overall, there would be gender balance among the 75 total interviewees. Accordingly, 20 applicant interviewees were female, and 5 were male; 20 were Caucasian, and 5 were African American.

Limitations of interview sample. Of the 75 total interviewees, 38 were female, and 37 were male; 68 were Caucasian, and 7 were African American. The underrepresentation of people of color plagues both the field of practice and research in educational administration overall. It is certainly a limitation of this case study. I addressed that limitation by supplementing case study data with syntheses of other scholars' previous research specific to people of color in educational administration. However, as noted in Chapter 4, prior research also tends to focus on African Americans, rather than all people of color, in school leadership.

It is also important to note that New York City was not included in the original case study. New York City (with its 32 community districts, citywide Chancellor of Schools, special regulations for administrative licensure, and unique sociopolitical context) is governed in such a distinct way from the other 709 districts throughout the state that it merits a separate study of its own. Interestingly, even the State Education Department typically reports its statistical profiles in two groups: New York City and "Rest of State" (SED, 1997).

Other limitations. Both the literature reporting prior studies and the original research shared here do not address many aspects of diversity that can be relevant to accessing the superintendency. For example, issues related to sexual orientation, religion, disability, and other potentially important differences remain unexamined, providing fertile territory for future research.

Interview focus and context. The substance of the interviews for this study focused on respondents' recent firsthand experiences in conducting (in the case of headhunters and school board members), applying for, or considering applying for superintendency vacancies (in the case of candidates). Interview protocols were only partially structured, allowing respondents to introduce unanticipated directions as they recounted their experiences. I typically began with broad, open-ended inquiries about the nature of their previous involvement with superintendent searching and hiring. If it did not emerge naturally in the course of these discussions, I later introduced probes encouraging comparisons of different searches and perspectives on issues related to gender and ethnic/racial diversity in the search process.

Examples of the kinds of inquiries made include the following: Tell me what recruitment and screening were like in the last superintendent search you facilitated. Talk about how the board made its decision to hire its last two superintendents. What was the nature and source of any advice you received about pursuing a particular superintendent opening? What were exploration, application, and interviewing processes like the last time you participated in a superintendent search? What else haven't we talked about that your experience tells you is important to understanding how school administrators obtain a superintendency? What, if anything, can you tell me about the participation of women or people of color in your most recent search?

Participant Observation Fieldwork

In addition to the 75 interviews, I conducted participant observations in more than a dozen different settings relevant to the focus of this study. Each produced a rich set of fieldnotes that became supplementary data for the case.

For example, I attended an open forum where three semifinalist candidates answered questions from interested community and staff members in a particular district about to hire a new superintendent. I attended five public school board meetings where the superintendent search was part of the formal agenda.

I also attended several relevant conferences. For example, I spoke with audience members and presenters at a full-day statewide conference for aspiring superintendents. This is an annual event sponsored by (among others) the state association of school superintendents and geared to promoting interest in the superintendency. Most participants in this event are nominated by incumbent superintendents, although some self-select to attend.

Similarly, I attended six separate 1- to 2-hour sessions dedicated to the topics of "Acquiring a Superintendency," "Is the Superintendency for You?" and "Searching and Selecting a Superintendent." These sessions were part of various professional development opportunities offered intermittently and sponsored by the state school board association, the state superintendents' association, or the state association of women school administrators.

Slightly more indirectly related to my research focus, I also participated in a full-day statewide conference aimed at exploring the future of the superintendency. This forum assembled more than 100 incumbent superintendents and engaged them in small-group problem solving around a wide range of current issues. The questions addressed in that setting that were most related to this research were the following: How do we attract the best and the brightest to our profession? What kind of preparation or experiences are needed, for experienced or inexperienced superintendents, to ensure success? How can we raise the image of the superintendency? What can be done to improve and stabilize the relationships between school boards and superintendents?

I also participated in nine 2-hour meetings of an ad hoc task force charged with the task of studying the issue of women and minorities' representation in the superintendency in New York State. This 11-member committee was appointed by the 38 regional superintendents' group and operated over the course of 3 years.

All of the information gleaned from these observations in the field helped provide additional context for the data derived from individual interviews. Also, this fieldwork provided the opportunity for informal conversations with which to compare and contrast data from the 75 research interviews.

Document Analyses

In addition to the literature review, fieldwork in the observational settings just described were also rich sources of additional documents that shed light on the research focus. For example, presenters at these conferences and forums routinely provided handouts, synopses of their remarks, background materials, and copies of articles they had written that were germane to these issues. These documents carried titles such as "So You Want to Be a Superintendent?" (authored by an incumbent superintendent); "Getting That First Superintendency," "Stock Interview Questions to Expect," "The Resumé and Credentials," and "Sample Interview Questions" (authored by several different search consultants).

Consultants, school board members, and candidates also gener-
ously shared written materials related to their search experiences.
These included samples of agendas and promotional materials from
regional initiatives to interest experienced administrators in the superintendency, vacancy announcements and brochures advertising
openings for school superintendents, packets of materials that consultants share when training interview teams and school boards for
questioning candidates, surveys and questionnaires used to elicit
community and board members' preferences regarding candidate
qualifications and background experiences, proposals and market-
ing materials that headhunters create to compete for boards' selection as the consultant of choice, and forms used by headhunters to
summarize data about applicants.

Final Remarks on Research Methods

In sum, both original case study data from recent investigations
in one state and previous research conducted in other states and nationally were integrated to present the composite presented in the
body of this volume. The case study was comprehensive in scope, including data from documents, fieldwork, and interviews. The perspectives and experiences of those closest to superintendent search
and selection practices were relied upon, including school board
members, headhunters, and applicants.

References

Afton, D. (1985). *The development of models of educational consultants' perceptions of the executive search process.* Unpublished doctoral dissertation. Syracuse University, Syracuse, NY.

Ashforth, B., & Mael, F. (1989). Social identity theory and the organization. *Academy of Management Review, 14,* 20-39.

Bailey, S. (1998). Different questions: Better answers. *Educational Researcher, 27*(9), 13.

Baker, J. (1952, October). Selection of superintendents. *Phi Delta Kappan, 34,* 6-7.

Baltzell, D. C., & Dentler, R. A. (1983). *Selecting American school principals: A sourcebook for educators.* Cambridge, MA: ABT.

Bank, B. (1997). Introduction: Some paradoxes of gender equity in schooling. In B. Bank & P. Hall (Eds.), *Gender, equity and schooling: Policy and practice* (pp. 3-29). New York: Garland.

Banks, C. M. (1995). Gender and race as factors in educational leadership and administration. In J. A. Banks & C. A. McGee Banks (Eds.), *Handbook of research on multicultural education* (pp. 65-80). New York: Macmillan.

Barker, S. (1997, November). Is your successor in your schoolhouse? Finding principal candidates. *NASSP Bulletin,* pp. 85-91.

Bell, C. S. (1988). Organizational influences on women's experience in the superintendency. *Peabody Journal of Education, 65*(4), 31-59.

Bell, C. (1995). "If I weren't involved with schools, I might be radical": Gender consciousness in context. In D. Dunlap & P. Schmuck (Eds.), *Women leading in education* (pp. 288-312). Albany: SUNY Press.

Bell, C., & Chase, S. (1993). The underrepresentation of women in school leadership. In C. Marshall (Ed.), *The new politics of race and gender: Yearbook of the Politics of Education Association* (pp. 141-154). Washington, DC: Falmer.

Bell, C., & Chase, S. (1996). The gendered character of women super-intendents' professional relationships. In K. Arnold, K. Noble, & R. Subotnick (Eds.), *Remarkable women: Perspectives on female talent development* (pp. 117-131). Cresskill, NJ: Hampton.

Berman, J. A. (1997). *Competence-based employment interviewing.* Westport, CT: Quorum.

Biklen, S. K., Bogad, L., & Luschen, K. (1996, April). *Feminism and the lives of girls in schools: Scholarship, method, and change.* Paper presented at the annual meeting of the American Educational Research Association, New York City.

Bjork, L. (1993). Effective schools—effective superintendents. *Journal of School Leadership, 3,* 246-259.

Black, J., & English, F. (1986, 1996). *What they don't tell you in schools of education about school administration.* Lancaster, PA: Technomic.

Blount, J. (1998). *Destined to rule the schools: Women and the superintendency 1873-1995.* Albany: State University of New York Press.

Bredeson, P. (1996). Superintendents' roles in curriculum and instructional leadership: Instructional visionaries, collaborators, supporters, and delegators. *Journal of School Leadership, 3,* 243-264.

Brown, M. (1992). Only the best. *American School Board Journal, 179*(3), 35-36.

Byrne, D. (1971). *The attraction paradigm.* New York: Academic Press.

Campbell, R., Cunningham, L., Nystrand, R., & Usdan, M. (1990). *The organization and control of American schools* (6th ed.). Columbus, OH: Merrill.

Carlson, R. O. (1961). Succession and performance among school superintendents. *Administrative Science Quarterly, 6,* 210-227.

Carlson, R. O. (1972). *School superintendents: Careers and performance.* Columbus, OH: Merrill.

Carter, G., & Cunningham, W. (1997). *The American school superintendent: Leading in an age of pressure.* San Francisco: Jossey-Bass.

Carter, D., Glass, T., & Hord, S. (1993). *Selecting, preparing, and developing the school district superintendent.* Washington, DC: Falmer.

Castallo, R., Fletcher, M., Rosetti, A., & Sekowski, R. (1991). *School personnel administration: A practitioner's guide.* Boston: Allyn & Bacon.

Castetter, W. B. (1996). *The human resource function in educational administration* (6th ed.). Englewood Cliffs, NJ: Merrill.

Catalyst. (1996). *Women in corporate leadership: Progress and prospects.* New York: Author.

Chase, S. (1995). *Ambiguous empowerment: The work narratives of women school superintendents.* Amherst: University of Massachusetts Press.

Chase, S., & Bell, C. (1990). Ideology, discourse, and gender: How gatekeepers talk about women superintendents. *Social Problems, 37*, 163-177.

Chase, S., & Bell, C. (1994). How search consultants talk about female superintendents. *School Administrator, 51*(2), 36-42.

Chion-Kenney, L. (1994). Search consultants: Boon or bane to nontraditional candidates for the superintendency? *School Administrator, 51*(2), 8-9, 12-15, 17-18.

Cistone, P. (1982). School boards. In L. Mitzel (Ed.), *Encyclopedia of educational research* (5th ed., Vol. 4, pp. 1637-1645). New York: Free Press.

Clark, D., & Astuto, T. (1986). The significance and permanence to changes in federal education policy. *Educational Researcher, 15*(8), 3-14.

Corwin, R., & Borman, K. (1988). School as workplace: Structural constraints on administration. In N. Boyan (Ed.), *Handbook of research on educational administration* (pp. 209-238). New York: Longman.

Crowson, R. (1987). The local school district superintendency: A puzzling administrative role. *Educational Administration Quarterly, 23*(3), 49-69.

Cuban, L. (1988). *The managerial imperative and the practice of leadership in schools*. Albany: State University of New York Press.

Cullen, K. (1995). Literature review findings: Evaluation of superintendents. *Journal of Personnel Evaluation in Education, 9*, 351-367.

Danzberger, J. P., & Usdan, M. D. (1992). Strengthening a grassroots American institution: The school board. In P. F. First & H. J. Walberg (Eds.)., *School boards: Changing local control* (pp. 91-124). Berkeley, CA: McCutchan.

Dipboye, R. (1992). *Selection interviews: Process perspectives*. Cincinnati, OH: Southwestern.

Doughty, R. (1980). The Black female administrator: Women in a double bind. In S. Biklen & M. Brannigan (Eds.), *Women and educational leadership*. Lexington, MA: Lexington Books.

Dovidio, J., Kawakami, K., & Johnson, C. (1997). On the nature of prejudice: Automatic and controlled processes. *Journal of Experimental Social Psychology, 33*, 510-540.

Dunlap, D., & Schmuck, P. (Eds.). (1995). *Women leading in education*. Albany: State University of New York Press.

Edson, S. K. (1988). *Pushing the limits: The female administrative aspirant*. Albany: State University of New York Press.

Edson, S. K. (1995). Ten years after: Too little, too late? In D. Dunlap & P. Schmuck (Eds.), *Women leading in education* (pp. 36-48). Albany: State University of New York Press.

Education Vital Signs. (1997). *American School Board Journal, 184*(12), A15.

Ehrlich, E., Flexner, S. B., Carruth, G., & Hawkins, J. (1980). *Oxford American dictionary.* New York: Oxford University Press.

Ferguson, K. (1984). *The feminist case against bureaucracy.* Philadelphia: Temple University Press.

First, P. F., & Walberg, H. J. (1992). *School boards: Changing local control.* Berkeley, CA: McCutchan.

Glass, T. (1992). *The 1992 study of the American school superintendency.* Arlington, VA: American Association of School Administrators.

Glass, T. (1993). Through the looking glass. In D. Carter, T. Glass, & S. Hord (Eds.), *Selecting, preparing, and developing the school district superintendent* (pp. 20-36). Washington, DC: Falmer.

Gleaves-Hirsch, M. (1997, September 28). Council takes on racism. *Syracuse Herald American,* pp. B1, B7.

Greene, M. (1998). Moral and political perspectives: The tensions of choice. *Educational Researcher, 27*(9), 18-19.

Grogan, M. (1996). *Voices of women aspiring to the superintendency.* Albany: State University of New York Press.

Grogan, M., & Henry, M. (1995). Women candidates for the superintendency: Board perspectives. In B. Irby & G. Brown (Eds.), *Women as school executives: Voices and visions* (pp. 164-175). Austin: Texas Council for Women School Executives.

Half, R. (1985). *Robert Half on hiring.* New York: Plume.

Hennig, M., & Jardim, A. (1977). *The managerial woman.* Garden City, NJ: Anchor Press.

Hodgkinson, H., & Montenegro, X. (1999). *The U.S. school superintendent: The invisible CEO.* Washington, DC: Institute for Educational Leadership.

Holdaway, E., & Genge, A. (1995). How effective superintendents understand their work. In K. Leithwood (Ed.), *Effective school district leadership* (pp. 13-32). Albany: State University of New York Press.

Hord, S., & Estes, N. (1993). Superintendent selection and success. In D. Carter, T. Glass, & S. Hord (Eds.), *Selecting, preparing, and developing the school district superintendent* (pp. 71-84). Washington, DC: Falmer.

Houston, P. (1998, June 3). The ABC's of administrative shortages. Education Week on the Web, 17(38), pp. 44, 32. Available: www.edweek.org

Hoyle, J. (1993). *Professional standards for the superintendency.* Arlington, VA: American Association of School Administrators.

Hudson, M. (1994). Women and minorities in school administration: Re-examining the role of informal job contact systems. *Urban Education, 8,* 386-397.

Institute for Educational Leadership. (1986). *School boards: Strengthening grassroots leadership.* Washington, DC: Author.

Jackson, B. (1995). *Balancing act: The political role of the urban school superintendent.* Washington, DC: Joint Center for Political and Economic Studies.

Jackson, B., & Cibulka, J. (1992). Leadership turnover and business mobilization: The changing political ecology of urban school systems. In J. Cibulka, R. Reed, & K. Wong (Eds.), *The politics of urban education in the United States* (pp. 71-86). Washington, DC: Falmer.

Johnson, C. (1975). How to select a superintendent. *American School Board Journal, 162*(11), 28.

Johnson, S. M. (1996). *Leading to change: The challenge of the new superintendency.* San Francisco: Jossey-Bass.

Kamler, E. (1995). *Gatekeeping: The relationship between the search consultant, women, and the superintendency.* Unpublished doctoral dissertation, Hofstra University.

Kamler, E., & Shakeshaft, C. (1998, April). *The role of search consultants in the career paths of women superintendents.* Paper presented at the annual meeting of the American Educational Research Association, San Diego.

Kanter, R. M. (1977). *Men and women of the corporation.* New York: Basic Books.

Konnert, M. W., & Augenstein, J. J. (1990). *The superintendency in the nineties: What superintendents and board members need to know.* Lancaster, PA: Technomic.

Kowalski, T. (1995). *Keepers of the flame: Contemporary urban superintendents.* Thousand Oaks, CA: Corwin.

Krinsky, I. (1992). Cream of the crop. *American School Board Journal, 179*(6), 34-37.

Krupp, J. A. (1983). How to spark an aging staff: Some suggestions. *Illinois School Research and Development, 20*(1), 38-46.

Krupp, J. A. (1991). Beyond the 3 R's: Focusing on quality life. *Journal of Staff Development, 12*(4), 20-30.

Leithwood, K. (Ed.). (1995). *Effective school district leadership: Transforming politics into education.* Albany: State University of New York Press.

Levine, S. (1989). *Promoting adult growth in schools: The promise of professional development.* Boston: Allyn & Bacon.

Linn, M. (1998). When good intentions and subtle stereotypes clash: The complexity of selection decisions. *Educational Researcher, 27*(9), 15-16.

Magowan, C. (1979). *The contribution of nationally recognized consultants to the practice of selecting a superintendent.* Unpublished doctoral dissertation, University of Connecticut.

Maienza, J. (1986). The superintendency: Characteristics of access for men and women. *Educational Administration Quarterly, 22*(4), 59-79.

Marietti, M., & Stout, R. (1994). School boards that hire female superintendents. *Urban Education, 8*, 373-385.

Marshall, C. (1985). The stigmatized woman: The professional woman in a male sex-typed career. *Journal of Educational Administration, 23*, 131-152.

Marshall, C. (1997). Undomesticated gender policy. In B. Bank & P. Hall (Eds.), *Gender, equity, and schooling: Policy and practice* (pp. 63-91). New York: Garland.

Martin, T. (1978). *A study of the procedures and processes utilized in the selection of a superintendent of schools.* Unpublished doctoral dissertation, University of Illinois at Champaign-Urbana.

Maruca, R. (1997). Workplace equity: Says who? *Harvard Business Review, 75*(6), 15-16.

McAdams, R. (1998). Who'll run the schools: The coming administrator shortage. *American School Board Journal, 185*(8), 37-39.

McCarthy, M. M., & Kuh, G. D. (1997). *Continuity and change: The educational leadership professoriate.* Columbia, MO: University Council for Educational Administration.

Meet the powerbrokers. (1994). *School Administrator, 51*(2), 20-23.

Miklos, E. (1988). Administrator selection, career patterns, succession, and socialization. In N. Boyan (Ed.), *Handbook of research on educational administration* (pp. 53-76). New York: Longman.

Montenegro, X. (1993). *Women and racial minority representation in school administration.* Arlington, VA: American Association of School Administrators.

Moody, C. (1983). On becoming a superintendent: Contest or sponsored mobility? *Journal of Negro Education, 52*, 383-397.

Natale, J. (1992, December). Up the career ladder. *Executive Educator,* pp. 16-21.

New York State School Boards Association [NYSSBA]. (1988). *Selecting the superintendent: A handbook for school board members.* Albany: Author.

New York State School Boards Association [NYSSBA]. (1995). *The school board member handbook.* Albany: Author.

Norton, S., Webb, L., Dlugosh, L., & Sybouts, W. (1996). *The school superintendency: New responsibilities, new leadership.* Boston: Allyn & Bacon.

O'Connell, R. W. (1995). *A report of the status of the administrative candidate pool in New York State—1995.* Albany: New York State Council of School Superintendents.

O'Connell, R., & Tallerico, M. (1998). *Gender analyses: A second look at Snapshot III survey data on New York State superintendents* [Research monograph]. Hudson: New York State Association for Women in Administration.

Ortiz, F. I. (1982). *Career patterns in education: Women, men, and minorities in public school administration.* New York: Praeger.

Ortiz, F. I. (1991). An Hispanic female superintendent's leadership and school district culture. In N. Wyner (Ed.), *Current perspectives on the culture of school.* Cambridge, MA: Brookline.

Ortiz, F. I. (1998, April). *Seeking and selecting Hispanic female superintendents.* Paper presented at the annual meeting of the American Educational Research Association, San Diego.

Ortiz, F. I., & Marshall, C. (1988). Women in educational administration. In N. Boyan (Ed.), *Handbook of research on educational administration* (pp. 123-141). New York: Longman.

Ortiz, F. I., & Marshall, C. (1995). Becoming a school leader: The case of females and minorities. *People and Education, 3*(1), 83-110.

Ortiz, F. I., & Ortiz, D. (1995). How gender and ethnicity interact in the practice of educational administration: The case of Hispanic female superintendents. In R. Donmoyer, M. Imber, & J. Scheurich (Eds.), *The knowledge base in educational administration: Multiple perspectives.* Albany: State University of New York Press.

Pigford, A., & Tonnsen, S. (1993). *Women in school leadership: Survival and advancement guidebook.* Lancaster, PA: Technomic.

Radich, P. (1992). *Access and entry to the public school superintendency in the state of Washington: A comparison between men and women.* Unpublished doctoral dissertation, University of Washington.

Rebore, R. (1991). *Personnel administration in education: A management approach* (3rd ed.). Boston: Allyn & Bacon.

Rickabaugh, J. (1986). *The role and influence of consultants in the selection of school superintendents.* Unpublished doctoral dissertation, University of Wisconsin.

Riehl, C., & Byrd, M. (1997). Gender differences among new recruits to school administration: Cautionary footnotes to an optimistic tale. *Educational Evaluation and Policy Analysis, 19*(1), 45-64.

Roberts, M. (1996). *The role of executive search consultants in the selection of school superintendents.* Unpublished doctoral dissertation, Virginia Polytech.

Robinson, G., & Bickers, P. (1990). *Evaluation of superintendents and school boards.* Arlington, VA: Educational Research Service.

Rose, R. (1969). *Career sponsorship in the school superintendency.* Unpublished doctoral dissertation, University of Oregon.

Rosse, J., & Levin, R. (1997). *High-impact hiring: A comprehensive guide to performance-based hiring.* San Francisco: Jossey-Bass.

Rush, S. (1998). Why can't you see her? *Outlook, 91*(4), 4-7.

Scheurich, J., & Young, M. (1998). In the United States of America, in both our souls and our sciences, we are avoiding white racism. *Educational Researcher, 27*(9), 27-32.

Schmuck, P. (1981). The sex dimension of school organization: Overview and synthesis. In P. Schmuck, W. Charters, & R. Carlson (Eds.), *Educational policy and management: Sex differentials* (pp. 221-233). New York: Academic Press.

Schmuck, P., & Dunlap, D. (1995). Introduction. In D. Dunlap & P. Schmuck (Eds.), *Women leading in education* (pp. 1-8). Albany: State University of New York Press.

Schmuck, P., & Wyant, S. (1981). Clues to sex bias in the selection of school administrators: A report from the Oregon network. In P. Schmuck, W. Charters, & R. Carlson (Eds.), *Educational policy and management: Sex differentials* (pp. 73-97). New York: Academic Press.

Schneider, A. (1998). *A study of superintendent residency requirements in New York State.* Unpublished report, State University of New York at Brockport.

Shakeshaft, C. (1989). *Women in educational administration.* Newbury Park, CA: Sage.

Shakeshaft, C. (1995). Foreword. In D. Dunlap & P. Schmuck (Eds.), *Women leading in education* (pp. xi-xvii). Albany: State University of New York Press.

Shakeshaft, C. (1998). Wild patience and bad fit: Assessing the impact of affirmative action on women in school administration. *Educational Researcher, 27*(9), 10-12.

Skrla, L. (1998, April). *The social construction of gender in the superintendency.* Paper presented at the annual meeting of the American Educational Research Association, San Diego.

Starratt, R. (1996). *Transforming educational administration: Meaning, community, and excellence.* New York: McGraw-Hill.

State Education Department [SED]. (1997). *New York, the state of learning: Statewide profile of the educational system.* Albany: Author.

Sullivan, W. (1997). *Human resources for small businesses.* New York: Wiley.

Swart, W. (1990). *A comparison of three models used by local school boards in New York State to assist in the superintendent selection process 1975-1990.* Unpublished doctoral dissertation, New York University.

Tallerico, M. (1989). The dynamics of superintendent-school board relationships: A continuing challenge. *Urban Education, 24,* 215-232.

Tallerico, M. (1997). Gender and school administration. In B. Banks & P. Hall (Eds.), *Gender, equity, and schooling: Policy and practice* (pp. 187-210). New York: Garland.

Tallerico, M., & Burstyn, J. N. (1996). Retaining women in the superintendency: The location matters. *Educational Administration Quarterly, 32,* 642-664.

Tallerico, M., Burstyn, J. N., & Poole, W. (1993). *Gender and politics at work: Why women exit the superintendency.* Fairfax, VA: National Policy Board for Educational Administration.

Tallerico, M., Poole, W., & Burstyn, J. (1994). Exits from urban superintendencies: The intersection of politics, race, and gender. *Urban Education, 8,* 439-454.

Tannen, D. (1990). *You just don't understand: Women and men in conversation.* New York: Ballantine.

Tieman, P. (1968). *A survey of educational consultants and their role in the recruitment and selection of school superintendents.* Unpublished doctoral dissertation, Ohio State University.

Tyack, D., & Hansot, E. (1982). *Managers of virtue: Public school leadership in America: 1820-1980.* New York: Basic Books.

U.S. Bureau of the Census. (1997). *Statistical abstract of the U.S., 1997* (117th ed.). Washington, DC: Author.

Van Nostrand, C. H. (1993). *Gender-responsible leadership: Detecting bias, implementing interventions.* Newbury Park, CA: Sage.

Volpe, R., Archambault, P., Barretta, A., Service, R., Terranova, M., & Whitehill, W. (1998). *Snapshot of the superintendency III: A study of school superintendents in New York State.* Albany: New York State Council of School Superintendents.

Webb, L. D., Montello, P., & Norton, M. S. (1994). *Human resources administration: Personnel issues and needs in education* (2nd ed.). New York: Merrill.

Wheatley, M. (1979). *The impact of opportunity and power structures in schools: Why women don't become school administrators.* Cambridge, MA: Goodmeasure.

Wheatley, M. (1981). The impact of organizational structures on issues of sex equity. In P. Schmuck, W. Charters, & R. Carlson (Eds.), *Educational policy and management: Sex differentials* (pp. 255-271). New York: Academic Press.

Wrubel, S. (1990). *Superintendent succession: Needs, selections, and changes in four New York public school districts.* Unpublished doctoral dissertation, Fordham University.

Yeakey, C., Johnston, G., & Adkison, J. (1986). In pursuit of equity: A review of research on women and minorities in educational administration. *Educational Administration Quarterly, 22*(3), 110-149.

Zakariya, S. B. (1987). What you get (and what you pay) when you hire a superintendent search service. *American School Board Journal, 174*(11), 35, 37-38.

Zeigler, L., & Jennings, M. (1974). *Governing American schools: Political interaction in local school districts.* North Scituate, MA: Duxbury.

Index

**CORWIN
PRESS**

The Corwin Press logo—a raven striding across an open book—represents the happy union of courage and learning. We are a professional-level publisher of books and journals for K–12 educators, and we are committed to creating and providing resources that embody these qualities. Corwin's motto is "Success for All Learners."